THE ART OF

COMING

HOME

Craig Storti is available as a trainer/consultant in the subjects covered in this book. He can be reached at

e-mail: cstorti@carr.org

Phone: 410-346-7336

Fax: 410-346-7846

Craig Storti is also the author of

Americans at Work: A Guide to the Can-Do People

The Art of Crossing Cultures

Cross-Cultural Dialogues: 74 Brief Encounters with Cultural Difference

Figuring Foreigners Out

Incident at Bitter Creek

Old World/New World: Bridging Cultural Differences

THE ART OF
COMING
HOME

CRAIG STORTI

INTERCULTURAL PRESS
A Nicholas Brealey Publishing Company

BOSTON • LONDON

This edition first published by Intercultural Press, a Nicholas Brealey
Publishing Company, in 2003. For information contact:

Intercultural Press, Inc.
a division of
Nicholas Brealey Publishing
100 City Hall Plaza, Ste. 501
Boston, MA 02108 USA
Tel: (+) 617-523-3801
Fax: (+) 617-523-3708
www.interculturalpress.com

Nicholas Brealey Publishing
3–5 Spafield Street
Clerkenwell
London EC1R 4QB, UK
44-207-239-0360
Fax: 44-207-239-0370
www.nbrealey-books.com

First published by Intercultural Press in 1996

Cover design: Ken Leeder

ISBN-10: 1-931930-14-7
ISBN-13: 978-1-931930-14-7

Printed in the United States of America

10   09   08   07   06   8   9   10   11   12

**The Library of Congress has
previously catalogued this edition as follows**

Storti, Craig.
    The art of coming home/Craig Storti
        p.   cm.
    Includes bibliographical references.
    ISBN 1-877864-47-1
    1. Reverse culture shock.   2. Repatriation.   3. Social adjustment.   4. Cross-
cultural orientation.   I. Title.
    GN517.S74   1997
    302.'14—dc21   96-35182
                                                                              CIP

Dedication

To Joseph Coyle and
Sally Di Paula
for helping us home

Table of Contents

Figures

The Phaeacian sailors deposited the sleeping Odysseus on the shore of Ithaca, his homeland, to reach which he had struggled for twenty years of unspeakable suffering. He stirred and woke from sleep in the land of his fathers, but he knew not his whereabouts. Ithaca showed to him an unaccustomed face; he did not recognize the pathways stretching into the distance, the quiet bays, the crags and precipices. He rose to his feet and stood staring at what was his own land, crying mournfully: "Alas! and now where on earth am I? What do I here myself?"

—Homer
The Odyssey

Acknowledgments

Anyone who writes on readjustment is automatically in Clyde
Austin's debt, not only for his excellent book of readings but also
for the many treasures in his extensive archives at Abilene Christian University. While their encouragement alone would have been
a great boon, Clyde and Sheila Austin also shared their archives,
time, and hospitality with me. If books can have godparents, then
the Austins played that role for this volume.

I can never get far into an acknowledgments page without
thinking of Sandra Fowler and Fanchon Silberstein. In the present
instance, both Sandy and Fanchon shared their considerable resources with me, for which I am grateful, but I also want to thank
them for their ongoing support and encouragement over the years.

I had a lot of help with chapter 5. Bettina Hansel and David
Bachner sent me useful articles on exchange students and talked
with me at length on the telephone. Sydney Hickey, Anne Tarzier,
and Randy Eltringham opened my eyes to military reentry. For the
missionary section I relied heavily on David Pollock, and was likewise well served by Lynn Tyler and William Taylor. At the Peace
Corps, Mona Melanson gave me the idea (and some of the items)
for the list that became Figure 5.1. Other help along the way came

from Laurette Bennhold-Samaan, Dawn Kepler-Betts, Robert Harris, Lee Lacy, Bruce La Brack, and Norma McCaig.

David Hoopes made me work much harder on this book than I ever intended to, but no harder than I should have. I am, as always, deeply grateful to him, to Kathleen Hoopes, and to Judy Carl-Hendrick for making me look so much better in print.

Through no fault or shortcoming of their own, people like those mentioned above can only be of intermittent help to an author. One's wife, on the other hand, is there for the duration, constantly making room in the marriage for a book. For that and so much more, thank you, dearest C.

Introduction

When I go back I know I shall be out of it; we fellows who've
spent our lives out here always are.
  —Somerset Maugham *The Gentleman in the Parlour*

It is a well-known fact that living and working overseas take some getting used to. Cultural adjustment is a much-studied and increasingly well-understood phenomenon. Books have been written about it and people regularly attend workshops and seminars to learn how to cope with it. In a sure sign the phenomenon has arrived, the phrase "culture shock" has been plucked from its origins in the intercultural field and is now commonly used by the man in the street to describe adjusting to any difficult or unexpected set of circumstances.

With the front end of the overseas experience so well discussed and documented, it's surprising to find that the back end, coming home, has received relatively little attention. After all, most of the people who go overseas eventually come back. Yet, few books on readjustment are available, and training seminars on the subject are still very much the exception rather than the rule—even among those same companies and organizations that spend good money preparing people to go overseas.

None of this would make any difference, of course, if reentry were as simple as most people expect—merely a matter of picking up where you left off. But all the evidence, both anecdotal and statistical, confirms that it is in fact a complicated and usually difficult experience. Indeed, most expatriates find readjusting back home, now commonly known as reverse culture shock, more difficult than adjusting overseas ever was. Consider:

- In one study of American returnees, 64 percent reported "significant culture shock" upon repatriation.
- In another survey, 64 percent of Dutch and 80 percent of Japanese expats said they found coming home more difficult than adjusting overseas.
- Only 7 percent of returning teenagers said they felt at home with their peers in the United States.
- More than 50 percent of Swedish exchange students said they "didn't fit in" when they returned to Sweden.
- Seventy-five percent of returning soldiers in one study said they found reentry "difficult, time-consuming, and acrimonious."
- More than 50 percent of the executives in a survey of U.S. corporations said they experienced social reentry problems upon repatriation.

When you think of the number of people temporarily living and working overseas at any one time—such as expatriate business people and their families, government and military personnel and their families, exchange and study-abroad students—nearly all of whom are eventual returnees, the case for helping people understand and deal with readjustment becomes even stronger. Using the United States as an example, at any given time nearly 2.5 million Americans are in residence overseas (excluding permanent residents of foreign countries), at least a quarter of whom are likely to return home each year. Other countries may have even higher numbers (or at least a higher percentage of their overall population).

The reentry arithmetic becomes even more compelling when you consider that readjustment has been found to have a profound impact not only on the returnee but also on family members, colleagues, and close friends. When you add all of the figures together, the worldwide number of people significantly affected at any one time by the phenomenon of reentry must be in the millions.

And all indications are that the number of would-be returnees is growing, especially in the private sector, as globalization becomes a fact of business life. Over one hundred thousand U.S. companies now do business internationally, for example, and more than twenty-five thousand of these companies operate offices abroad. Patric Oster has observed in his article, "The fast track leads overseas," in *Business Week* magazine,

> *Globalization means more managers must make stops abroad. General Motors Corp. has 485 U.S. managers overseas, up 15 percent from 1991. Gerber Products Co. is thinking of tripling [its] number. Likewise, Motorola Inc. [has] expanded its rank of senior executives overseas by 10 percent and plans another 10 percent increase. "We expect it to continue to increase as a reflection of the fact that markets are opening up overseas," says a Motorola spokesman.* (1993, 64)

The case for paying attention to readjustment is supported by yet another set of numbers: the financial costs. It has been estimated that it costs the average company roughly the equivalent $250,000 U.S. a year in salary, benefits, and subsidies to keep an expatriate and his or her family in an overseas assignment. With an average overseas stay of three to four years, the investment in the employee adds up to nearly a million dollars.

That's all right, of course, as long as the employee stays with the company and the investment is recouped, but the statistics here are also not very encouraging.

- Twenty-five percent of returnees leave their parent company within one year of coming home.
- Twenty-six percent of returnees were actively looking for another job.
- Forty-five percent of companies surveyed reported "problems with attrition" among returnees.
- Seventy-four percent of returnees did not expect to be working for the same company one year later.
- Two-thirds of returning professionals complained of suffering from the "out of sight, out of mind" syndrome upon reentry.

Employees leave their organizations for many reasons, of course, and people who don't go abroad also move on, but the most common reason for returnee attrition is dissatisfaction with the position the employee is assigned upon reentry. It's interesting to note in this context that while two-thirds to three-quarters of companies in the United States offer some kind of orientation for employees heading abroad, only 28 percent have a repatriation program for returnees. This seems backwards, for surely the greater risk to the organization is not the expat who doesn't work out overseas—and is normally reabsorbed into the company back home—but the successful expat who comes home only to become the frustrated returnee who then leaves the company altogether. The fact that approximately "one in four returning expatriates leave their firm...represents a substantial financial and human capital loss," Stewart Black and Hal Gregersen have observed,

> especially if the skills, knowledge, and experience that the individual gains are important to the firm and scarce in the internal or external labor markets. Thus, the practical reasons for investigating the repatriation adjustment process

seem as compelling as those for understanding expatriate cross-cultural adjustment. (1991, 672)

Behind all these numbers are people, of course, many of whom are wondering what's happening to them. Let's listen in for a moment.

It was very nice to come back and see the people and get settled.... But all of a sudden, I went from this position of being a manager [overseas] and having virtually complete control over what I did and what the people did who worked for me to being just one of the people here again—having a director sitting twenty feet away and two managers sitting even closer to me. I was answerable to all three, after having no boss at all.
—American businessman

My job description did not even exist when I came home. I felt as though I had no status in the company. In fact, everybody was asking, "Hey, what are you doing here."
—Finnish expatriate executive

When I got back, I found I was no longer a round peg in a round hole, but a square peg trying to find a hole that didn't seem to be there at all.
—New Zealand aid worker

When I got back to my hometown in Ohio and went to work, I fell back into hanging out evenings in the neighborhood tavern with my old buddies. After about two weeks of that I gave up the tavern. They didn't care about the problems of the Indians in Peru, and I didn't give a damn what happened to the Indians in Cleveland.
—American Peace Corps volunteer

People pushed and shoved you in New York subways or they treated you as if you simply didn't exist. I hated everyone and everything I saw here and had to tell myself over and over again, Whoa, this is your country, it is what you are part of.

—American college student

Coming back home was more difficult than going abroad because you expect changes when going overseas. It was real culture shock during repatriation. I was an alien in my home country. Old friends had moved, had children, or just vanished. Others were interested in our experiences, but only sort of. They simply couldn't understand.

—Finnish expatriate spouse

Everyone seemed unfriendly and snobbish. It was impossible to break into the right cliques and make friends. Clothes mattered more than personality, and competition was tremendous. The activities through which I was expecting to meet people weren't as easy to get involved in as I'd thought they would be. People did seem to go to parties every weekend, just like in the movies, but I was never invited. I knew no one and it was fairly obvious they did not want to know me.

—American teenager

I knew what I had to do. I didn't say the ice cream was awful, even though I said it to myself. I said to my friends, "Quito is wonderful." They [invite] me to go to parties, but I am not enthusiastic.

—Ecuadorian exchange student

We came from a lovely rural area of England to the Los Angeles area. We were in an apartment and knew no one. Our son's bike was stolen and we had roaches. I reacted the same way I did when I arrived in Korea: I didn't go out and I wouldn't let the boys out. I felt threatened.

—American military spouse

My advice about coming home? Don't.

—Japanese businessman

In this book we will consider the key issues of the phenomenon of reentry and offer suggestions—for returnees, their family and friends, and employers—for dealing successfully with this experience. Chapter 1 examines what we might call generic reentry, the most common issues returnees face regardless of what they were doing overseas, their role in the family, or what they will be doing upon their return. Chapter 2 explores the stages of reentry and describes how returnees can expect to feel as they pick their way through this transition. Chapter 3 looks at the return to the workplace, the issues employees face upon reentering their organization after an overseas sojourn. Chapter 4 considers the return of spouses, young children, and teenagers—issues specific to these three groups (and not treated in chapter 1). And chapter 5 examines four special populations: exchange students, international foreign aid volunteers, military personnel and their families, and missionaries and missionary children.

   We realize, of course, that there are as many experiences of reentry as there are people coming home, that every returnee could write his or her own book and no two of those volumes would be alike. There is reentry after a year overseas, after two, after four. There is reentry from a country you loved and hate to leave, and from a country you did not enjoy and are happy to turn your back on. There is reentry from a country radically different from your own and from a country quite similar to home, from developed countries and from developing countries. There is voluntary and involuntary reentry, expected and totally unexpected reentry, premature and delayed reentry. There is reentering at age thirty, with children, and at age fifty-five, as grandparents. There is your first reentry, your second, and your fourth. You may return to the same house you left and the same job, or you may return to a different part of your home country and to a different job. Or to no job at all. There is the reentry of people who were running away from home and of expatriates who went abroad kicking and screaming. And there are cultural differences, too; the reentry of a Japanese family to Japan won't be the same as the reentry of a German family to Germany or an American family to the United States.

Reentry, in short, is a deeply personal experience and a cultural one as well. While we have tried to select and discuss the most common concerns of most returnees in most countries, no single returnee will have exactly the experience we describe in these pages, and some will have experiences that are not mentioned here. Even so, we expect most returnees will recognize themselves repeatedly in this volume.

While returnees themselves will be the most avid readers here, loved ones, friends, employers, and colleagues of returnees will likewise find a great deal to ponder in these pages. To the extent that their lives are affected by what returnees go through during reentry, family, friends, and others can only be helped by having their own understanding of the experience. To the extent they may want to help returnees through the experience—or at least not make it harder for them—such understanding becomes essential. "I [had] two trips and two experiences [when I went] abroad," one returnee noted. "The [overseas] trip influenced me. The [return] influenced everyone around me."

We close with a caveat: Readers of this book could be forgiven for concluding that an overseas experience doesn't stack up very well against the apparent heartache of reentry, that unless one's sojourn abroad is extraordinarily rich, it could never compensate for the problems of coming home. But this is not at all the message here. Reentry, for all its minor and a few major annoyances, can't begin to diminish the lustre of an expatriate experience. Indeed, it is in some ways precisely because the overseas experience is so rich and stimulating that reentry becomes a problem. In other words if you are having trouble readjusting, it's probably because you had such a terrific time abroad.

Moreover, simply because reentry can be frustrating, lonely, and generally unpleasant at times is not to say that it is a harmful experience or a negative one. After all, frustration, loneliness, and unpleasantness are very often the precursors of insight and personal growth. Maybe reentry doesn't always feel good, but then feeling good isn't much of a standard for measuring experience.

Make no mistake about it; reentry *is* an experience to be reckoned with, but when the reckoning is done and the accounts are cleared, you are likely to find that the price you paid for your overseas sojourn was the bargain of a lifetime.

1

Coming Home

I had to be hungry—starving!—they decided, so they took
me to the restaurant first. "So, wild man, tell us about
Africa," they said. "Were you living with savages or what?"
*   I was really hungry, eating all the bread, and wonder-*
ing how square pieces of butter had fallen into my dish of
extra ice.

— "Bush Pigs" Richard Dooling

Why should coming home be so difficult? You have missed this place and these people, after all, and have looked forward to being back here for months. You've always had a wonderful time when you visited on home leave or passed through on business. So why is it so anticlimactic? Why does most of the pleasure seem to have come in the anticipation and not in the reality? Why would you give anything to be back overseas again when you have been home less than a week? What's wrong with you anyway?

It's a question often asked by returning expatriates. "I couldn't have been more excited," Nancy Koehler, a U.S. Navy spouse, remembers.

After two and one-half years living in Japan, I was on an airplane and on my way home. Blissful thoughts about being back in the U.S.A., long-awaited visits with family and friends outweighed any nostalgia I felt.... My every thought told me everything back home was going to be perfect and problem-free.

This euphoria was short-lived, however. Within a few weeks I found myself, unexpectedly, in the depths of despair instead of at the anticipated peak of ecstasy. Instead of enjoying the company of old friends and neighbors, I couldn't seem to find anything to talk to them about. Instead of enjoying driving on wide and familiar roads, I was petrified because I often found myself on the wrong side of them. Instead of enjoying supermarket shopping, I was overwhelmed by the quantity and the variety of items available.

What was wrong with me? Here I was truly "back home," where I had dreamed of being for our entire overseas tour; yet I was miserable—lonely, afraid, confused, depressed, lethargic. I didn't care whether the moving boxes ever got unpacked, even the ones containing our carefully chosen Japanese treasures. What had happened? (in Austin 1986, 89–90)

As a matter of fact, nothing very unusual. Koehler, like most people who live overseas and then come home, was just going through what is known as reentry, or reverse culture shock. Not only is reverse culture shock quite normal, most returnees say that readjusting after coming home is much harder than adjusting to the "foreign" country ever was. The only difficulty, of course, is that while expatriates expect living overseas to take some getting used to, they imagine coming home to be a matter of course. When it isn't, when it turns out to be even harder than adjusting abroad, they're surprised and confused.

But the question persists: Why is it so hard to come home? The answer to this question has many parts, but the biggest by far concerns the notion of home and the expectations it sets up in us. To truly understand reentry, we need to understand what we mean by home, what we want—and especially what we need—home to be. Once we have understood the real meaning of home, we can examine reentry from that perspective. And then we will begin to see why this transition can be so difficult.

The Issues

The Meaning of Home

As it happens, *home* has several meanings, at least two of which do in fact describe this place you have come back to, but the third and most important of which is rather wide of the mark. In the sense that home is the place where you were born and raised, where people speak your native language and behave more or less the way you do—what we might call your home*land* and your home culture—then it is indeed home that awaits you as you step off the jumbo jet. If you should happen to think of home only in this limited sense and expect nothing more of it, then the place you return to will not disappoint you.

But this is not in fact what most people mean by home— which is where all the trouble starts. Most people use the word in a more profound sense, referring to a set of feelings and routines as much as to a particular place. In this formulation home is the place where you are known and trusted and where you know and trust others; where you are accepted, understood, indulged, and forgiven; a place of rituals and routine interactions, of entirely predictable events and people, and of very few surprises; the place where you belong and feel safe and secure and where you can accordingly trust your instincts, relax, and be yourself. It is,

3

in short, the place where you feel "at home."

"Home is not merely the homestead," Alfred Schuetz has written in his essay "The Homecomer,"

> my house, my room, my garden, my town—but everything it stands for.... "To feel at home" is an expression of the highest degree of familiarity and intimacy. Life at home follows an organized pattern of routine; it has its well-determined goals and well-proved means to bring them about, consisting of a set of traditions, habits, institutions, timetables for activities of all kinds. Most of the problems of daily life can be mastered by following this pattern. There is no need to define or redefine situations which have occurred so many times or to look for new solutions of old problems hitherto handled satisfactorily. The way of life at home governs as a scheme of expression and interpretation not only my own acts but also those of other members of the in-group. I may trust that, using this scheme, I shall understand what the other means and make myself understandable to him.... I have always a fair chance...to predict the other's action toward me as well as the other's reaction to my own social acts. We not only may forecast what will happen tomorrow, but we also have a fair chance to plan correctly the more distant future. Things in substance will continue to be what they have been so far. (1945, 370–71)

These are much broader definitions, of course, though much closer to what most people expect and require of home. Needless to say, they are also a much higher standard by which to measure the place you have returned to—a standard, in fact, that any such place cannot possibly meet. As we will see, this very realization, that home is really not home, is at the core of the experience of reentry.

Let us look more closely at this meaning of home, then, and apply it to the place you have returned to. For simplicity's sake, we can reduce the essence of home as described above to three key elements:

1. familiar places
2. familiar people
3. routines and predictable patterns of interaction

While separate and distinct to some extent, these three elements also have a causal relationship, with routines and predictable interactions depending very much on the presence of familiar places and people. And all three, in turn, make possible most of the feelings we associate with home—security, understanding, trust, safety, and belonging—listed above. How, then, does the place returnees come back to, the place they insist on calling home, measure up to these three criteria?

Familiar Places. One of the first things you notice about home is that familiar places aren't quite so familiar anymore. While there will be many things you recognize (assuming you return to your previous place of residence), any town or city is bound to have changed in your absence. There will be new streets, new traffic lights, new buildings and shopping centers, perhaps even whole new neighborhoods. Some old buildings may have been torn down or may now be occupied by a different tenant; many shops, restaurants, and other services will have moved or closed; the post office, cinema, bank, or hospital may be in a new location; some old roads go to places they never used to and some new ones turn up in places where they shouldn't be. There's a carpark where your doctor's office used to be and an office building in the city center where you used to park. Clearly, you can't come back to your town or city and rely only on your instincts to get from one place to another. It may be home, but you are going

5

to have to learn how to get around all over again.

Even your old street may have changed. The house next to you has been renovated and painted a different color, and the house on the other side has a new garage (which makes your dining room dark). The old oak tree in front of your apartment building came down in a thunderstorm last year and your living room is much more exposed than it used to be. Meanwhile, a hedge at the rear has grown so tall that your kitchen no longer has a view of the park. The place just doesn't feel the same.

There may be other, subtler changes to your neighborhood, as Marcia Miller found out when she came back after teaching a year in China. "It did not take long to notice a marked change in my neighborhood," she writes,

> a change that shocked and alienated me. It had always been an upper-middle-class area; now it was clearly just upper class. Prior to my departure for China, housing prices had been creeping up gradually, but I had not paid attention as that increase was a reflection of overall inflation. However, during the year I had been away, property values had soared.... As an offshoot of this real estate madness, cannibalistic rents had driven out many of the established shops that catered to the residents' practical needs. Those shops were replaced by expensive clothing boutiques guarded by armed men. Many new people lived in my building who did not say hello to me. These people were clearly in a different income bracket than I. Riding in the elevator with them, I felt like a poor cousin temporarily boarding in a rich aunt's home. Although I knew we could easily afford the modest increase in our monthly maintenance charges, I did not want to reside there. In a word, I was distinctly uncomfortable in my home environment and I had no hope of changing it. (1988, 14)

The same people aren't in the same places anymore either. Your next-door neighbors have moved, and you don't recognize half the faces you meet as you walk down your own street. There's a new teller at the bank, your old barber has retired, the helpful woman at the bookshop got a new job, your favorite pharmacist moved to another city, and the corner convenience store has all new clerks. A large part of what makes familiar places familiar, that contributes to that underlying feeling of belonging and well-being, is the presence of people who recognize you and whom you recognize; in this regard home is clearly lacking. It's hard to feel you belong in a place where half the people you meet ask you where you come from.

Even if you recognize many of the places of home, they aren't going to feel the same to you as they did before you left, not because they have changed but because you have. You will not have the same emotional associations or connections with many of the places that used to loom large in your life, places that used to "mean something" to you for whatever reason. Or you may now see the same places differently. What once seemed clean to you now seems dirty, or vice versa. A place where you liked to jog is now unappealing because of traffic or noise. A lovely park now seems like little more than an urban intersection. Taking your children to the zoo is depressing after visiting the game parks of Africa. The sidewalks feel impossibly crowded or eerily empty. The traffic is overwhelming. Part of what makes a place familiar is the feelings it evokes in you, and now, after a long absence and numerous life-changing experiences, you won't feel the same about many of the places from your past.

"Wherever it lies, the country is our own," Malcolm Cowley has written.

Its people speak our language, recognize our values....

This is your home...but does it exist outside your memory? On reaching the hilltop or the bend in the road, will you find the people gone, the landscape altered, the hemlock trees cut down and only stumps, dried tree tops, branches, and fireweed where the woods had been? Or, if the country remains the same, will you find yourself so changed and uprooted that it refuses to take you back, to reincorporate you into its common life? (1991, 117–18)

Some returnees come back to their home country but to a town or city that is different from the one they lived in before going abroad. This place won't look familiar, of course, but then neither are these people expecting it to, which may actually make their readjustment easier. As we will see throughout this book, much of the sting of reentry is not so much that things are different—we learn to handle the different quite well when we go overseas—but that we are expecting them to be the same.

For all these reasons, then, home is not that collection of familiar places you are expecting and not, therefore, a place where you are likely to feel you belong, at least not in the beginning.

Familiar People. The second expectation of home is that the people, like the places, will also be familiar, not in the sense that you recognize them but in the deeper sense that they have not changed appreciably while you were gone and will not regard you as having changed either. And you expect, therefore, that you will be able to have essentially the same relationships with these people that you had before you went away. In other words, you assume that time stopped while you were abroad.

This is unlikely. The people of home, you will soon discover, have changed almost as much as the places. The changes will be of two kinds: external and internal. The former are the more obvious and the easier to grasp. A few people may have died;

some others may have married, divorced, or become parents; still others have become sick or senile; some have moved away, moved across town, or moved in with someone new; some have changed jobs, companies, or careers; some former best friends now have new best friends made in your absence. Everyone is older.

But even people who live in the same place, are married to the same person, and work in the same job are not the same people you knew when you went away. They have had two or three years of experiences that have altered who they are, experiences and alterations you know nothing about. Time hasn't stopped for them anymore than it has stopped for you, though it has indeed stopped for both of you as far as shared experiences with the other are concerned. Relations with intimates change "entirely for the [person] who has left home," Schuetz writes.

> To him, life at home is no longer accessible in immediacy. He has stepped, so to speak, into another social dimension [isolated from] the scheme of reference for life at home. No longer does he experience as a participant in a vivid present the [events] which form the texture of the home group. His leaving home has replaced these vivid experiences with memories, and these memories preserve merely what home life [was] up to the moment he left it behind. (372)

Home, to be precise, may include many familiar faces, but it contains very few familiar people. You won't be able to pick up where you left off with loved ones and friends nor take any of your relationships for granted. You won't be able to relax entirely and be yourself, trusting to your instincts, nor will they be able to relax and be themselves around you. You will all have to come to know each other again. "Having grown personally in another culture," a New Zealand foreign aid worker remembers,

I found it difficult to adapt back to a situation that now seemed less ideal. This was not a bad thing, and meant in fact that one carved out a new position for oneself, in terms of relationships with people who were significant— but the reassessment on both sides was difficult at times.

Routines and Predictable Interactions. Routines are the third hallmark of home. A routine is anything you do without thinking, without paying conscious attention to your actions and words; indeed, in its purest form a routine is something you do while you are paying conscious attention to *something else.* A routine can be a sequence of behaviors, like shaving or driving, or a ritual conversational exchange where in a particular setting you always say the same things to the same people and they say the same things back. Many routines are a combination of the two, a predictable and unchanging sequence of behaviors accompanied by a never-varying sequence of conversational exchanges. Some of the things we do are not entirely routines but have certain routine elements. Riding a bicycle would be a routine behavior for most adults—they wouldn't have to think how to do it—but riding a bicycle on a busy, dangerous highway or during a thunderstorm would contain a number of nonroutine elements. Certain parts of conversations are routine, greetings and leave-takings, for example, but not others. Nor is a greeting always routine, such as the first time you greet someone in French or Arabic.

Routines clearly depend on the familiar and the known, in terms of places and people. Shaving or putting on makeup, for example, may not be quite so routine in a hotel as it is in your own bathroom. Nor is greeting a stranger as much of a routine as greeting your spouse. If it were not for routines, if everything you did and said required your conscious attention, you would be overwhelmed by the minutiae that make up most behavior and therefore could accomplish very little. It is because of routines that the mind can be confronted with the new and the unfamiliar and not fall apart; the unconscious goes about its routines while the conscious attacks the problem of the new (and eventually may turn that into a routine).

Because of routines, the predictability of so much of what you do, you feel in control much of the time and able to relax; you can trust your instincts and be yourself. Routines also enhance your sense of well-being and security and thereby contribute to feelings of self-confidence and self-esteem.

Anyone who has been an expatriate knows that routines get mightily disrupted when you go overseas, where almost everything and everyone is new and unfamiliar. Indeed, during the early days of adjusting abroad, you spend most of your conscious energy and time merely creating new routines, leaving higher-order functions for later. For example, you don't know where anything is, inside or outside the home, or how to do the most "routine" things, like driving, cashing a check, perhaps even going to the bathroom (in the land of Turkish toilets). This disappearance of routines explains that common expatriate phenomenon in which otherwise mature adults can get so excited about successfully mailing a letter or completing a telephone call.

Coming home, as we have seen above, you are surrounded once again by unfamiliar places and people (albeit much to your surprise) and with much the same effect as when you went abroad: routines are disrupted and you have to create new ones before you can feel settled. In the meantime, nothing comes naturally. The most mundane tasks once again require your conscious attention, and most of your interactions with people, even close friends and loved ones, will be somewhat awkward and uncomfortable, at least until you can verify whether and how they may have changed while you were gone and what they may think about the new you. You are continually on edge, not able to trust your instincts and just be yourself.

Thus far, home isn't doing very well, having failed all three of our important tests. It is manifestly not that land of familiar places, people, and routines you were counting on, having in fact become surprisingly *un*familiar while you were away—so much so that upon your return, you must actually learn to adjust to home. This means, of course, that it can't really be home at all, for if home is anything, it is certainly a place you should not have to get used to.

Home As a Foreign Country

Part of the reason home doesn't measure up, then, is because it has changed so much in your absence. The other part, of course, is that you have changed so much as a result of your overseas experiences, and the person you have now become will inevitably not see home the same way as the person who went overseas two or three years ago. Indeed, whether home itself actually changed at all while you were away, it is bound to appear changed to you because of your new perspective on it. "The reasons for reentry shock have to do with change," Judith Martin has written, "change within the home environment itself during the period of the individual's absence and change within the individual as a consequence of [one's] stay abroad. The severity of reentry shock is related to the magnitude of [these] changes" (1984, 123). While you may recognize some of the features of home, you will find others surprising, offensive, and even shocking. You will respond to your homeland much the way a stranger would, and for the same reason—because you are now an alien in your own country.

How does it happen that you can become a stranger in your own land? The answer involves what occurs when a person moves overseas and adjusts to a foreign country. Adjusting to another culture is a process that begins with the encountering of all manner of behaviors and living conditions that are different from what one is used to back home, running the gamut from quaint or odd on up to confusing, frustrating, disgusting, and just plain wrong. Such a state of affairs, which results in what is generally known as culture shock, cannot go on for long or we would soon cease to function. While we humans can tolerate a certain amount of novelty and confusion, if nothing in our environment is familiar or understandable, then even the most routine behaviors become impossible.

Indeed, in the beginning of an overseas sojourn, when you are overwhelmed by the new and different, you do cease to function so far as many higher-order behaviors are concerned and simply concentrate on surviving. Over time, after you have established a few routines and thereby rendered certain aspects of your life predictable and controllable, you begin to get used to more and more (but not all) of the unusual behaviors and living conditions you find around you. In the case of the behaviors, you even start to adopt a few. These phenomena, the way people act and the circumstances of daily life, gradually become norms, and you begin to expect—and therefore, to *depend* on—them. They define what you begin to consider normal, and their certainty and predictability make it possible for you to relax and feel comfortable and to go beyond mere coping or surviving. In due course, you find yourself judging new behaviors and circumstances using these norms as the standard. So it is that behaviors and conditions that confused or frustrated you a few short months ago now form part of your value system. Gary Weaver has written of this process.

> As we adapt overseas, we become comfortable with our
> new physical and social environment. The food, weather,
> buildings, people, music, and ways of interacting become

familiar. We find life more predictable and know what to expect from others and what they expect from us. We learn how to get things done, solve problems, greet people, accept gifts, give tips, negotiate prices, and determine appropriate social roles. All of these...ways of doings things are often [called] cues or reinforcers. [And it is] the absence of home-culture cues that make[s] us feel like fish out of water until we adjust to new ones in the overseas culture. (1987, 5)

Examples of the kinds of adjustments expatriates make, both general and specific, abound. Depending on the culture you come from, you may adjust to a slower pace of life overseas or to a faster one, to a culture where people are more demonstrative than back home, freely showing their feelings, or where people never show their true feelings, always keeping an impassive exterior. You may get used to a more group- or family-oriented social structure or to a more individual-centered one, to more or fewer creature comforts and to a less or more materialistic society. You may adjust to a more direct or indirect communication style, a less or more time-conscious mentality, and a more or less results-oriented worldview. The norm in your new culture may be to take a two-hour lunch and work until 7:00 P.M., to never talk business at a first meeting, and to take wine with dinner. People in your new culture may feel that it is wrong to question authority, that bosses should be autocratic, and that subordinates shouldn't take the initiative. You also adjust to not having and not doing many of the things you had and did back home and to having and doing all manner of new things in the foreign country. Expats from Japan and from urban areas in Europe often have to get used to much larger living quarters and homes with front and backyards.

Whatever the norms, you adjust to them, and in the process you gradually make a home out of the foreign country. This is quite natural, of course, for as we noted above, the need for home—for those feelings of safety, security, and belonging that home provides—is deep and compelling and is thus not likely to somehow be suspended when you move overseas. Rather, one goes about creating precisely that land of familiar places, people, and routines discussed earlier. It's not surprising that one's "real" home undergoes something of a transformation in the process.

What happens, then, when you come home? Wherever you turn, you are confronted by behaviors and circumstances that now seem as different to you as many of those you encountered when you first arrived abroad. From the perspective of your new norms, home is now strange, and you react in much the same way as you did when you got to Brazil or Taiwan: you find much of your environment confusing, frustrating, disgusting, and just plain wrong. "Returnees," Weaver notes in the same article, "miss the cues and reinforcers they [got used to] overseas" (5). It is, as we have already noted, culture shock in reverse. While there may be a voice in the back of your mind telling you that this doesn't make sense, that these are the same behaviors and circumstances you once found normal, you can't help reacting the way you do. Back from her year in China, Marcia Miller took her first walk through the streets of New York. "It was a hot, sultry day," she writes.

15

> *The park was mobbed with people in all states of dress, wearing clothes that people in Daqing reserve for their beds. I was appalled at people's emotionalism. The overt physical expressions, especially between members of the opposite sex, stunned me. I stared at two people who greeted each other by screaming and embracing. It was so overdone, even hysterical. In Daqing, public behavior is circumspect, characterized by reticence.*

Walking on Broadway, I thought I was walking through a corridor in an insane asylum. I saw a Nordic type man, huge, covered with thick hair (the Chinese do not have much body hair).... A crowd at a busy corner surrounded two angry men who had squared off for a fight. Someone anxious to see the fight jostled me, throwing me off balance. The traffic was dense, the smog was consuming, and the noise, heightened by police sirens, was like a drill in my head. I was frightened. (13–14)

Chances are Miller did not react this way to many of these things before she went to China; indeed, she would not have noticed many of them. It was only their prolonged absence and their replacement in the interim by another set of routine behaviors and phenomena that caused these aspects of home to register now with such an impact. Virtually any behavior or living condition that is the opposite of what she had adjusted to in China would now shock or irritate her with its sudden reappearance. At the same time, the sudden disappearance of many now-familiar behaviors and phenomena in China would be troubling. In just this way, home—without changing much at all—becomes a foreign country to the returnee. "This can't be real life, I thought; this must be a show," Miller continues. "But it wasn't a show. This was urban life in America. I was perceiving other people according to my Chinese cultural 'lenses,' and I was horrified" (14).

While you may become accustomed to feeling out of place abroad, the strangeness of home is bound to be more alarming than the strangeness of overseas. You can accept that you are not going to fit in abroad in what is after all a foreign country, but the idea that you don't fit in back home, where you are in all likelihood going to spend much, if not the rest, of your life, is deeply disturbing. If you don't belong at home, then where do you belong?

16

It's not our intention here to catalogue all the "strangenesses" of home, but there are four we might linger over for a moment. For many returnees, people from developed countries in particular, there is often a strong reaction to how materialistic their society now appears, the sheer abundance and variety of material goods coming as something of a shock. How, for example, does a missionary family just back from two years in upcountry Malawi make sense out of the catfood aisle at the supermarket?

"I was incredulous at the prices...and the excess," one returnee observed.

The number of obese people, especially youngsters, shocked me. I was paralyzed by the sight of so much fresh food the first time I tried to shop. I had forgotten what was available in my city, five minutes from my home. There were not a few mounds of tired green vegetables lying on cement, but artistically arranged piles of gorgeously colored fruits and vegetables. The abundance, quality, and variety staggered me. There were three kinds of peppers—red, green, and yellow. There were four types of tomatoes— European, South American, local hothouse, and organic. I counted five kinds of berries. I could not trust myself to make a decision and left the store empty-handed.

A related shock, especially for those returning from lesser developed countries, is how this abundance is taken for granted and how much of it is wasted. "We don't use our resources to the ultimate extent," a returning foreign aid worker observed. "We have a piece of furniture for a while and then we just get tired of looking at it and go out and buy something new. We drive around in our cars senselessly, just to go for a ride. We are a very wasteful society."

The pace of life back home is another surprise for many returnees, especially those coming back to developed, industrialized countries. In many overseas posts, life unfolds at a stately, relaxed pace. There seems to be more time to do things (probably because there are fewer things to do), and people seem to have more time for each other, perhaps because there are fewer significant people in one's life. There's time to read, time for long leisurely dinner parties and extended conversation, and no such thing as a working lunch. Weekends are those two days when one doesn't go to the office.

Back home isn't like that. There are responsibilities one didn't have overseas—taking care of the house, family obligations—and the children's lives suddenly seem amazingly busy. The day is packed, evenings are scheduled, and weekends are a blur. Life is hectic (if not especially full). "Someone had turned up the volume and speeded up the film," one returnee observed. "[The whole country] was in a hurry. Everybody talked, walked, and ate as if there were a prize for the fastest."

It is not only behaviors that strike one differently, but people's values and attitudes, especially toward other countries and cultures. Living overseas makes many expatriates more conscious of the world beyond their country's borders, and they are also used to mingling with people with a similar broad perspective. By contrast, the people back home often seem narrow and provincial. "Finns still think they live in the center of the world," one returnee observed, "and the rest of the world doesn't exist." Often the people one knows back home can't talk about world affairs, hardly even national affairs, and see no reason why they should know about other countries. In the worst cases, they seem downright prejudiced, even xenophobic. "I was talking to people who didn't know where Poland was," one Peace Corps returnee recalls. "They had such a small-town mentality. They just felt no connection to what I was interested in." For someone who now fancies him- or herself a citizen of the world, this insularity can be a letdown.

Needless to say, the idea of adjusting to such a culture, the spectre of actually becoming like these people, is not instantly attractive. It's hard enough, under the best of circumstances, to be positive about home upon reentry, but when so much about home puts one off, readjustment is all the harder. "I tried to puzzle out [my] society," one returnee notes, "which I found incomprehensible. Perhaps it is more precise to say that I did not want to admit that I did understand it. I was horrified at what I understood and in disagreement with many of my society's basic premises. I did not want to be part of it." In time many expatriates discover that their own culture and people are not all quite as shallow, wasteful, shameless, and materialistic as they first appear, but initial impressions can be disappointing.

When you consider the changes that took place at home while you were abroad and throw in the changes that took place in you, it's no wonder coming home is not exactly the experience you were expecting. Indeed, because of these changes, "coming home" is in fact a practical impossibility and the phrase itself little more than a figure of speech.

None of this would matter very much, by the way, if you still had a home overseas—the precise location of home, after all, being much less important than the happy fact of having one. But there's the rub: even as you are busy discovering that your former home no longer fills the bill, your overseas home is already receding into memory. *To reenter, it turns out, is to be temporarily homeless.*

And homelessness is not pleasant. The reader will remember that we have been using *home* to mean the place where you belong and feel safe and secure and where you can accordingly trust your instincts, relax, and be yourself...the place where you feel "at home." The loss of home, accordingly, means the loss of just those feelings of safety and security, of belonging, of being able to relax and be yourself, the loss of part of your identity—all made more unpleasant by the fact that you were expecting to feel precisely the opposite. No wonder reentry takes some getting used to. Alfred Schuetz has written,

> *The homecomer expects to return to an environment [where] he [had] always had and—so he thinks—still has intimate knowledge and which he has just to take for granted in order to find his bearings. [While] the approaching stranger has to anticipate in a more or less empty way what he will find, the homecomer has just to [return] to the memories of his past. So he feels, and because he feels so, he will suffer the typical shock described by Homer [in The Odyssey]. (369)*

To be sure, this place you have arrived in can *become* home again, even as it once was before you went abroad, but in the meantime it will feel very much like a foreign country. And coming home, consequently, will feel suspiciously like culture shock.

It's Hard to Come Home

Charming. Could You Pass the Peas, Please? While the loss of home is probably the psychological and emotional centerpiece of reentry, there are a number of other issues returnees must also confront. Homelessness may play a part in many of these, but others are issues unto themselves. One of the most common complaints of returnees is how little interest the people back home show in their experiences, including close relatives and friends. Martha Gellhorn writes about her arrival back in England

> *Upon our return no one willingly listens to our travellers' tales. "How was the trip?" they say. "Marvellous," we say.*

*"In Tbilsi, I saw...." Eyes glaze. As soon as politeness per-
mits, or before, conversation is switched back to local news,
such as gossip, the current political outrage, who's read
what, last night's telly; people will talk about the weather
rather than hear our glowing reports on Copenhagen [or]
Katmandu. (1978, 11)*

This might not matter so much if you had just come back
from a week in the countryside or at the beach, but you have
been halfway around the world, seen places and done things these
people will never see and do, and you've been gone three or four
years besides. There's a lot to catch people up on.

Catching up is probably too simple a phrase to describe what's
going on here. The point of telling your stories, after all, is not
because you want to show off or because you crave attention but
because you realize that you are now something of a stranger to
friends and loved ones back home. You have been changed significantly by your experiences, and unless you can tell people
about them, how can they know this new person who has come
back to them? And if they can't know you, then what kind of
relationship can you now have with them? One expat writes,

*[I felt] dejection at not being able to communicate to oth-
ers the intensity of my China experience. I was expected to
be much the same person I was before going to China. But
I was no longer that person. I was so saturated with my
Chinese experience that I felt I was half Chinese. I may
have looked like the same blue-eyed, light-haired Westerner,
but a significant part of me had changed radically. I wanted
to discuss these changes and have them acknowledged.*

When you can't tell your stories, you are in effect obliged to
remain a stranger to the people you love. The keen sense of lone-

liness many returnees experience upon reentry comes from this feeling that close friends and relations no longer know who they are.

For some returnees, recounting experiences, especially the good ones, fills another important need: justifying the decision to move overseas in the first place. As far as your parents are concerned, for example, your decision to relocate halfway around the world, taking their grandchildren with you, may have been met with some skepticism, if not downright disapproval. It's self-indulgent, you might have been told, and probably unsafe besides. Colleagues may also have expressed some doubts, wondering if this was a good career move.

But you went anyway, of course, and upon coming home now feel a certain pressure to prove critics and skeptics wrong. So it is that you regale friends and loved ones with stories of great adventures and all of the other enriching experiences you and your children enjoyed abroad. Phrases like "the opportunity of a lifetime" and "I wouldn't have missed it for anything" will come readily to hand. But if you can't tell your stories, then you can never set the record straight.

I Thought These People Were My Friends

Why aren't people more interested? Part of the problem is the sheer amount of catching up that's needed. If you have been gone a long time, chances are you have a lot to tell. Most people can sit still and listen to your stories for half an hour or so, but after that their enthusiasm wanes. This doesn't mean they don't care about you anymore, only that their attention span, even for you, is limited. You shouldn't take it personally.

There's human nature at work here, too. Most of us are genuinely interested in other people, but at some point we expect them to return the favor and ask us a question or two. While it may be true that what has happened to you during the last two years is more dramatic and colorful than what has happened to loved ones back home, that doesn't necessarily make your stories more compelling. Hard as it may be to believe, their new job or new house is as interesting to them as your trip to Mt. Fuji was to you. And just as you are eager to fill them in on who you have become over the last two years, they would like to catch you up as well (when you've got a moment). Though they don't mean to, many expats leave the impression that they are the only ones who have been leading interesting lives, that whatever has happened back home could not, almost by definition, be as interesting as what happened overseas.

In some cases, those who stayed "behind" (note the expression) may feel threatened by you—or even jealous of your experience. They may resent that you had an opportunity they didn't have (though they wouldn't go overseas if their lives depended on it) or regret passing up a similar opportunity. Or you may make them feel inadequate or inferior by all you have seen and done. If you now speak a new language, this can make matters worse.

Friends and family members sometimes feel rejected and unappreciated if you carry on too much about how wonderful everything was overseas. If it was so wonderful, they may be thinking, and you liked it so much, then obviously you can't like being back here with them. If you should then make the additional mistake of comparing your experience abroad with home in unflattering terms, which is often how you feel about home when you first get back, your social circle will quickly become more circumscribed.

You Had to Be There

Even when people *are* interested (see Figure 1.1, pages 34–35, for ways other people can help you), they will not in every case be able to respond in the way you would like them to. If they have not had a particular experience, especially one that is out of the ordinary, it is not always possible for them to understand what you mean, to appreciate exactly what the experience meant to you, and to feel what you must have felt. "All too soon we shall be back among the crowds," the English adventurers Mildred Cable and Francesca French write in *The Gobi Desert*,

> *who, understanding nothing of its purpose, would measure [our] whole journey in terms of an adventure. They would certainly be interested and they would question us, but when we replied, they would be seeing it all from such a different point of view that the undertaking, as we viewed it, would be incomprehensible to them.* (1943, 287)

C. S. Lewis goes one step further and declares that even if people could understand, the problem is how to put some of these things into words (though he immediately proceeds to make an heroic attempt):

> *But what can one do with these scraps of information? I merely analyse them out of a whole living memory that can never be put into words, and no one in this world will be able to build up from such scraps quite the right picture. For example...how can one get across Malacandrian smells? Nothing comes back to me more vividly in my dreams...especially the early morning smell in those purple woods where the very mention of "early morning" and "woods" is misleading because it must set you to thinking of earth and moss and cobwebs...but I'm thinking of something totally different. More aromatic, yes, but then it is not hot or luxurious or exotic as that word suggests. Something aromatic, spicy, very cold, very thin tingling at the back of the nose—something that did to the sense of smell what high, sharp violin notes do to the ear. And mixed*

with that I always hear the sound of the singing—great hollow hound-like music from enormous throats, deeper than Chaliapin.... I am homesick for my old Malacandrian valley when I think of it. (1965, 155)

In the end returnees must accept that those who have not had an overseas experience can never understand things in quite the same way as those who have. This is finally true for almost any experience; we are all deeply subjective beings who, despite our ability to imagine and empathize, only truly understand the things that happen to us. All the same, in not being able to let others know what has happened to you overseas, some of the person you now are can never be known by friends and loved ones, and you may feel alien among them. "It might be," Cable and French wrote, "that after a time spent in an atmosphere of sophistication I, for one, should cease the mental struggle for expression and no longer try to convey my deeper thoughts about these desert experiences. In the end I might lock the door upon myself and even throw away the key" (287).

Home Is Not Abroad

Another feature of being back home is that you are trying to get used to not being overseas. You miss the friends you made, some of whom you may feel closer to than any of your friends back home. You may also miss the climate, the food, favorite amusements, old haunts. Perhaps you went to Venice or the Grand Canyon or Masai Mara game park for the weekend, whereas now the choices are the cinema, a concert, or your aunt's house. On vacation you may have skied in the Alps, climbed Kilimanjaro, or gone to Bali. Now your options are to visit your parents in Cincinnati or your sister down in Brighton. It's not that you don't like going to the cinema or won't enjoy seeing your sister; it's just that your leisure-time choices seem mundane and circumscribed. Life isn't as exciting as it used to be.

You may also miss the celebrity status many expatriates enjoy abroad. Outside of your home country, you automatically have a higher profile. You stand out because you are a foreigner; you are more interesting because you are a foreigner; you may be more sought after or listened to because you are a foreigner; you certainly get more attention because you are a foreigner. When you go to a party or a meeting, you may be the only person from your country at that event, which automatically makes you more interesting—and most expatriates enjoy the notoriety.

Back home you melt into the crowd; you are ordinary and anonymous again. No one turns to look at you, thinks your accent is quaint, marvels that you have come halfway around the world to live there. People don't find you interesting merely because you are from England or Italy. You can't dazzle people with your command of French, Swahili, or Chinese. You don't get invited to embassy parties or hobnob with the captains of industry. "In Gaeta [Italy], we were the big fish in the little pond," one navy officer recalled. "In Norfolk, we are just another gray hull amongst many." The writer V. S. Naipaul, of Indian ancestry but born and raised in Trinidad, captures the feeling here perfectly when he describes his first visit to India.

> *I was one of the crowd. In Trinidad to be an Indian was distinctive; in Egypt it was more so. Now in Bombay I entered a shop or a restaurant and awaited a special quality of response. And there was nothing. It was like being denied part of my reality. I was faceless. I might sink without trace into the Indian crowd. Recognition of my difference was necessary to me. I felt the need to impose myself, and didn't know how.* (1987, 43)

Your standard of living may plummet along with your celebrity status. Overseas you enjoyed the luxury of the beautiful company flat or the grand expatriate villa, complete with the cook, gardener, nanny, and watchman, something you could never afford if you were paying the rent. Back home, where you are paying, your own modest place doesn't quite measure up, and the only household help you know is your vacuum sweeper and electric clothes iron. "We're now living in a basement flat with our two kids," a Canadian returnee reported. "Our bathroom in Bamako [Mali] was bigger than our present living room. It's a real comedown, let me tell you." In one study, two-thirds of Japanese and 78 percent of Finnish returnees reported a reduced standard of living upon repatriation.

As your standard of living plummets, it usually takes your social status down with it. Overseas you may have effortlessly leaped several rungs in the social ladder and suddenly found yourself dining regularly with ambassadors, high government officials, popular cultural figures, and business leaders. At the same time, you entertained and played golf with generals or senior vice presidents from headquarters, people whose floor you weren't even allowed on when you worked back in Tokyo or London. Now you're happy when the neighbors accept your dinner invitations (after your parents said they were busy). "Another trouble that besets the [returnee]," Jean Boley has written,

> is that he has met celebrities while living abroad. He has been to parties at his Embassy and shaken the hand of several foreign secretaries and at least one Viceroy. No decent celebrity can have any idea of the damage he has inflicted upon the soul of, say, one Mortimer Small, Willow Grove, Idaho, by shouting at him through the cigarette smoke, "I say, you there, would you mind awfully passing

that plate of shrimps?" Nothing could seem more casual,
and yet in time it produces a periodic craving which we
call shrimpism, or a desire for a brush with famous people
at fashionable festivities. (in Austin, 67)

In the study mentioned above, more than half the Americans surveyed said they experienced a drop in social status upon re-entry.

Returnees often miss the closeness of the expatriate community. In many overseas posts the foreigners form close-knit networks of friends, people from the same country or company or from other countries with whom they share a common language and the status of being an expatriate. These people see each other regularly, either by design or because the expat community is so small they are always running into each other—at the international school, at the handful of stores that sell foreign foods, at the expat club, at any cultural event that is in one's native language. They are often at each other's homes for lunch and dinner, too, partly because entertaining is one of the few sources of expatriate amusement in some countries. It is very much like life in a small town.

Back home, people seem to lead more independent lives. They aren't thrown together so much, for one thing, and for another there are so many ways to amuse oneself that dinner parties or impromptu luncheons are far less frequent. Nor is there that implicit common bond, of being fellow foreigners, to prompt people to seek each other out. "The whole close environment at Fort Kobbe made me feel good and at home," one military spouse remembers. "Everyone seemed to care, but when I got back [home], I was very lonely because nobody seemed to care."

Perhaps what returnees miss most about being abroad is the sense of adventure and excitement, the stimulation of being surrounded by everything that is new and different. Daily life sparkles with exotic sights, out-of-the-ordinary experiences, new and sometimes profound insights into yourself and your own and the host culture, and the countless small triumphs that are part of learning how to function in a new country, a new culture, perhaps a new language. There is always something striking or unusual happening, and you seem to feel everything with an intensity absent in normal life. Experiences sometimes demand of you strengths or qualities that you didn't know you had, or had to that degree, or were obliged to develop on the spot. You can feel yourself growing.

Life back home can't match the intensity of life overseas (though it can have an intensity all its own, owing to the closeness you feel with loved ones). It isn't going to be a parade of exotic sights and mind-blowing experiences; insights won't be coming thick and fast; you won't find yourself tested so often; and personal growth is merely incremental. You miss acutely the challenges and the intense satisfaction of overcoming those challenges that are part of everyday life overseas. No less a personage than Henry Stanley, the intrepid *Chicago Tribune* journalist who finally found Dr. Livingstone in "deepest Africa," knew this feeling well. He wrote,

> *When a man returns home and finds for the moment nothing to struggle against, the vast resolve which has sustained him through a long and difficult enterprise dies away, burning as it sinks in the heart, and thus the greatest successes are often accompanied by a peculiar melancholy.* (in Spurling 1990, 368)

A young foreign aid worker returning after two years in Colombia was less eloquent but more succinct. "My problem," he said, "is that I'm twenty-three years old and I've already had the experience of a lifetime."

Some returnees don't manage their departure from abroad very well and feel the strain of having botched it. You may have forgotten to tell a certain person you were leaving or may not have allowed enough time to say good-bye to colleagues at work. Maybe a dear friend was on home leave or extended travel and you forgot to say farewell before that person left. There may have been odds and ends of business that didn't get resolved or a much-talked-about family trip to the rain forest that got put off until it was too late. You wanted to go one last time to a certain village, park, or restaurant—and it never happened. You talked about buying a Turkish carpet the whole time you were abroad, knew you had plenty of time, and now suddenly you're back home and you never got around to buying it. You quarreled with someone and you had to leave before you could patch it up. You meant to thank someone for a kind deed he or she did and the time just went by too fast. Not having left the overseas post in the way you meant makes it harder to come home the way you would like.

No Warning

Another feature of reentry is that it's all so unexpected. While the adjustments of reentry are real and troublesome enough, in many ways the shock of the experience is as much of a problem as the substance. Most expats know that living abroad is going to take some getting used to, and they prepare themselves accordingly. Most returnees, however, have no warning about reverse culture shock and neither expect it or prepare for it. While the typical expatriate hits the ground running, the typical returnee hits the ground and sinks immediately into the mire.

"When we anticipate a stressful event, we cope with it much better," Gary Weaver has noted. "We rehearse our reactions, think through the course of adjustment, and consider alternative ways to deal with the stressful event. We are prepared both physically and emotionally for the worst that could happen" (5). Expecting something doesn't guarantee that you will be ready for it, but it should blunt the impact somewhat. You may still stumble, but you will recover faster.

The problem is not just that reentry shock is unexpected, that the returnee is unprepared for the experience; the returnee is in fact expecting the exact opposite experience, that coming home will be quite wonderful. It's one thing to be taken by surprise; it's quite another to be taken *completely* by surprise.

Expatriates who have heard troubling rumors about reentry tend to discount them. How bad can it be, they think. After all, if I can get used to India, I can certainly get used to Brussels or Boston. Coming off the high of having learned a new language and figured out how to function and even triumph in a foreign country, they feel confident about anything life can dish up. While this confidence may help them navigate reentry better, it may also set them up for more of a jolt than they were expecting.

One Fell Swoop

Another factor which complicates reentry is that most of the issues surface simultaneously. You can't work on them one at a time, throwing all of your energy at the problem of uninterested relatives, for example, then regrouping and tackling the task of the jealous sister who now feels threatened by you.

In isolation most of the challenges of readjustment are quite manageable. The problem is that they don't occur in isolation, and the cumulative impact can be overwhelming. This fact, or rather ignorance of this fact, often causes returnees to underestimate themselves and to conclude they are handling readjustment more poorly than they are. They sense that they are falling apart and bemoan their lack of fortitude. If they could see an itemized list of what they were faced with, they would have a healthier respect both for what they're going through and for how well they're coping. The wonder wouldn't be that they were falling apart but that they hadn't done so sooner.

No One to Turn To

The loneliness of reentry may be the unkindest cut of all. In stark contrast to when you went overseas, where in all likelihood most of the people you met had gone through culture shock (the expatriates, anyway) and could help you through your adjustment, few or none of the people back home have gone through reentry. There is no one who understands what you're going through, no one to reassure you that the fears, doubts, anger, and pain you feel are perfectly normal, no one to promise you that you're really not losing your mind.

To make matters worse, chances are the important people in your life are wondering what all the fuss is about. Why aren't you enjoying being back home? (Don't you like us anymore?) Why do your moods swing so dramatically? Why are you so testy, depressed, and of all things, homesick? Why don't you just get on with your life? When you sense some of these sentiments in friends and loved ones, you feel pressure to get a grip on yourself and start being happy.

Worse still, many returnees, not understanding what they're going through either, wonder what *is* wrong with them. Why am I feeling like this? They put pressure on themselves to get over their discomfort, or whatever it is, and enjoy what ought to be a pleasant experience. This pressure, from without and within, only adds to their anxiety and self-doubt. "I wish I had been able to get in touch with friends who had shared my experience," one young woman recalls.

The problem was that those friends were in a different part of the country. The only friends I have in high school have never been abroad and can't understand these things. They couldn't understand this cultural shock. It seemed so fake to them that I was having trouble readjusting to my own culture.

The Practical Side of Coming Home

Where Do I Start? Coming home isn't all in the mind and emotions. There's also a nightmarishly long list of things you have to *do*, the practical side of reentry. You may have to find a new flat or buy a house, an enormously draining and time-consuming task under the best of circumstances. You may have to buy a car, another major undertaking at the best of times. You have to get the children in school, buy school clothes and supplies, arrange transportation. You have to open a bank account, get a credit card, take care of tax and insurance matters. Your sea freight hasn't come, has come too soon, or is missing key items. You need to hook up the phone, gas, electricity, and cable TV. You may have to get a driver's license, have your car inspected, change the license tags, and buy insurance. Various parts of your house or flat need scraping, painting, sanding, spackling, retouching, plastering, plumbing, wiring, cleaning, and just plain fixing. You have a lot of things to buy, unpack, put away, store, clean, and repair. There's a lot on your plate—and by the way, where are the plates?

Money Matters. Once you start doing some of these things, another reentry problem rears its ugly head: the question of money and, in particular, the lack of it. Consider the financial situation of the typical returnee: he or she has experienced a precipitous decline in salary, normally in the range of 30 percent (without the expat bonus), and has also lost many of the perks that expats come to take for granted—things like a company car and driver, company-paid club memberships (so you can meet the right

33

Figure 1.1
What Family and Friends Can Do

We have described what returnees can do to ease the pain of reentry, but what about family and friends? Here are a few ways they can make the transition back home smoother for you. (You might want to copy this list and give it to people.)

1. Show interest. Returnees very much need to share their experiences with you. They overdo it, of course, and show far too many slides (and never ask you about your life during the last two years), but try to be kind. They don't mean to be rude; they're just excited.

2. Don't be offended when they criticize their home country (which is also yours) and constantly compare it unfavorably with their overseas post. They don't include you in their sweeping generalizations, and they don't mean you're a fool to like it here, so don't get defensive. They're just on edge and a little lost. Just smile and offer them another helping of their favorite ice cream.

3. Don't make them feel defensive. Sometimes, by not understanding how hard reentry can be, you make returnees feel that there's something wrong with them, that they should be happy and content, that there's no reason they should be having a hard time. Even if you don't understand, act as if you do.

4. Don't pressure them to visit all the time. Parents and grandparents take note: give your loved ones some breathing room. Yes, it's rude of them not to come more often and stay longer, but at least they're back in the country!

5. Don't spring family problems and responsibilities on them too soon. No doubt it's time they started shouldering their family duties again, but give them a few weeks to get their balance.

Figure 1.1 (cont.)

6. Above all, be patient: They're not going to act like this forever. Whatever irritating, insensitive, disturbing, or alarming thing they do or say, don't take it too seriously. If they're still acting or talking like this after a couple of months, then you can start to worry.

---

people), paid home (vacation) leave, tuition reimbursements for the children's school, and free company housing. "When you return to your home country," one spouse observed, "lots of the benefits you were accustomed to disappear. It's like being Cinderella, and midnight has struck."

Meanwhile, prices have gone up at home, taxes are higher, and the children need new school clothes (which are not cheap). Worse, reentry involves a number of unusual, one-time expenses, such as getting a driver's license; joining the fitness club or the automobile club; getting shots for the dog; renting a second car; taking trips to visit loved ones; and buying new furniture and appliances. Your renters may also have left you with numerous repairs to be made to your flat or house. Phone bills skyrocket as your children call their friends in Paris or Santiago. And complicating everything, you don't know what your regular expenses are going to be yet, so you don't really have a fix on your disposable income. "Appliances, carpets, cars, day care, groceries, warm clothes...the expenses went on and on," Robin Pascoe remembers. "So did our 'budget discussions,' usually in an atmosphere so tense we could have marketed it for a new form of energy" (1992, 192).

Now That You're Back. Another practical matter you face now that you're home is the fact that friends, and especially family, may have some rather well-developed expectations of you. To begin with, they expect to see you a lot more often "now that there's no excuse," more often than you ever saw them before you went away. Grandparents may feel cheated that they haven't seen more of their grandchildren. And you can't use distance as an excuse; you may live in Milan or Osaka and your parents may live in Texas or London, but since you're back in the country, there's no reason your parents should have to wait until the next major holiday for a visit.

Family members may also expect you to start shouldering your share of family responsibilities again. Whether it's hosting Grandpa for the holidays, taking your turn to drive Aunt Mary to the south for the winter, or doing your share of the maintenance of the summer cottage on the lake, you're expected to do your part, maybe a little more to make up for all the time you were gone (and the rest of us had to do it for you!). At a time when you're only just managing to hold yourself—and, with luck, your family—together, to be handed responsibility for others somehow seems unfair.

Another truth about reentry is that family problems you left behind two or three years ago may be there waiting for you upon your return. They didn't go away simply because you did or resolve themselves in your absence, though you may have gotten that impression on quick visits home when the issues never surfaced. If you thought the issue had gone—or, worse, if you went away in part to escape from it—then there may be an unpleasant surprise waiting for you.

Home Leave Is Not Reentry

Returnees should be warned about the experience of home leave, those visits home while one is still living overseas. These are usually something on the order of idylls—near-perfect sightings of family and friends, short brushes with the best parts of your previous life—all lasting just long enough to remind you of everything that is good about home and none of what's not. They are genuine vacations, time out from real life, where nothing much matters because you don't live here anyway.

But these visits are in no way a preview of readjustment; in fact, they can be very misleading. Missing entirely from the home leave experience is that sense of homelessness that is at the core of reverse culture shock. Moreover, home leave is temporary and finite; it's going to be over in two weeks. Nor is reentry anything like time out from real life; it is, rather, the genuine article, not even remotely resembling a vacation.

What the Returnee Can Do

These, then, are some of the common problems of reentry, a rather long list as it turns out. Some are practical, where the only issue is finding the time, money, and energy to do what has to be done, and others are psychological and emotional, where the issue is to understand what is happening to you and what you are going through and why. In this section, we offer some suggestions for coping with the issues we have described above.

The first, assuming it's not too late, is to orchestrate a smooth departure. "Good-byes are important," Victor Hunter has written. "Without a meaningful good-bye, an effective closure, there cannot be a creative hello, a hopeful commencement" (1986, 179). Start planning your leave-taking several months ahead. Make a list of the people you want to be sure to say good-bye to and arrange for that to happen in due course. Decide what places you want to visit before you leave and make those arrangements, and buy those items you've always wanted but put off getting. In general identify personal and professional loose ends and tie them up. Coming home is burdensome enough; don't make it worse by leaving badly.

Another thing you can do while you're still overseas is to think about reentry. What exactly are you expecting to happen? How do you imagine it's going to feel? What assumptions are you making about how people are going to react to you, about the place you're going back to? What assumptions are you making about the people you left behind two years ago? Are you expecting them to have changed? What assumptions are you making about yourself? Do you assume you're the same person you were when you left London or Sydney? Get your assumptions and expectations out on the table and examine them. Chances are some of them will be quite astute, some others will be dubious, and a few will be downright amusing.

Probably the best thing you can do about readjustment is to be expecting it. As we noted earlier, the shock of reentry is almost as bad as the substance. While knowing it's coming won't change the particulars much—you'll still have to make the various adjustments—it will change the way you respond. You won't be caught off guard, and you will also have more realistic expectations of yourself, your family, and your friends. Reading about readjustment and, especially, talking to people who have been through it are probably the best ways to prepare yourself. But remember that being prepared won't make reentry painless, just less traumatic.

You should also remember that it's perfectly normal to find reentry trying and at times too much to manage, that there's nothing wrong with you just because you're depressed and want to go back overseas. Sometimes returnees think they're just going about it wrong, that if they only knew what other people knew, they would sail through the experience unscathed, that it's their fault they're having such a hard time. Relax. It's not you. You're not making this happen; it's there, waiting for you— and for everyone else who decides to come home.

It's also unwise to deny that you're having difficulty, to pretend that everything's going well and that you are as happy as your loved ones think you ought to be. You will feel pressure to do this at times, from those around you and from inside. You don't have to wear your frustration and disappointment on your sleeve, of course, but neither do you have to put on an act for anyone.

Don't jump to conclusions about your compatriots or otherwise despair too early in the game. This is probably not how you're always going to see them, as superficial and provincial, and not how they're always going to react to you—uninterested, threatened, and defensive. Remember, too, that part of how they behave may be in reaction to how you're coming across; if you're carrying on about how bad your own country is and how perfect Indonesia was, can you really expect people to keep asking you how it was it there? A little superiority goes a long way.

Another piece of advice here is to give yourself plenty of time to adjust. You're not going to feel at home for several weeks, even months. Transitions of this magnitude, complex and affecting so many parts of your life, are gradual affairs. Remember how long it took you to adjust overseas? Be patient—with yourself and with others.

Also remember that you have been through transitions before, perhaps not reentry per se but times when many things about your life changed and you had to adjust to a new set of circumstances. You did it, for example, when you went abroad, and you have done it every time you moved or changed jobs, when you got married (or divorced), when you had a child (or a child moved out), when a loved one passed away. Everyone is experienced in the disruptions and anxiety caused by life changes, and reentry is just the latest one. In other words, you already have most of the skills and instincts you will need to see you through the experience. It may be true, incidentally, that you have never been through a transition of quite this magnitude before, though the move abroad must have come close, but don't let that throw you. This is not an experience of an entirely different kind than you've had before; it's just on a different scale.

Practically Speaking

Clearly, most of what you can do about reentry involves adjusting your attitude and your expectations. There are, however, a few practical steps you can take to help you through the process. One is not to be so eager to tell everything that has happened to you all at once. While it is true that family and friends seem to have a limit on how much they can hear about your experiences, they may be more interested than you think—if you give them half a chance. You will be seeing these people again and again in the months to come; let your stories come out gradually. Mary Killen, advice columnist for the English weekly *The Spectator*, had some wise counsel to offer a concerned expat who wrote,

> *I am shortly to return from a most enjoyable six-week spell as writer-in-residence at Helsinki University. I am already worrying that I may bore or even alienate my friends in London by talking too much about Helsinki and Finland in general on my return. What would be the correct number of times I can mention these places on a daily basis?*
>
> A. B., Helsinki

> *Answer: If you limit your use of the words* Helsinki *and* Finland *to about a dozen times per day, you should run no danger whatsoever of alienating your English friends. Mention of "frozen sea" should be limited to five times a day; "reindeer meat" only once a day.* (1997, 63)

At the same time, you should be sure to ask the people back home what has happened in their lives while you were away, and then show at least as much patience for listening as they have shown you. They will be much more willing to hear about your life if you show an interest in theirs. "I was aware that I couldn't share [the experience] with most people," one New Zealand returnee recalled, "and erected a kind of non-committal barrier to protect myself, only to find that every now and again the most unlikely people would understand and ask intelligent questions."

Another useful strategy is to develop a budget as soon as possible, ideally while you are still overseas. Anticipate as many expenses as you can, both one-time and ongoing, and try to get a grip on what your take-home pay is going to be (and any other income you may receive). You won't be able to predict all of your expenses, especially the exceptional ones, or calculate exactly the ongoing expenses, but you should begin to get a sense of how much it's going to cost you to live back home. If income and expenses roughly balance, you may want to be cautious. If expenses win hands down, start thinking now about your priorities. What are the essential expenses which have to be met now and what are the ones that can wait?

In the same way, you should also prioritize the things you have to do, quite apart from the costs. Not all the tasks you face upon reentry have to be done right away. Maybe buying a commuter rail pass can't wait, but reupholstering the couch can. You may have to buy a car before too long, but meanwhile you can rent one for a few weeks. The flat does need painting, but you can still move in.

One of the most helpful things you can do during reentry is to seek out other returnees for a sympathetic ear. At times the burden of coming home seems too much to bear alone. There

41

must be people you met while you were abroad who returned ahead of you and whom you can now call or visit. Being able to talk to someone who understands what you're going through and who can validate the experience will be an immense emotional relief. There may not be such people in your community or in your immediate area, but don't let that stand in your way. At the same time there may be returnees in your community whom you don't know but whom you can call or to whom you can be introduced by mutual acquaintances. If you work for a large company, there are bound to be other people who have been posted overseas.

It's also possible to continue to have contact with foreigners even though you have come home. There may be international clubs or organizations you can join; you can sign up with your church, school, or civic association to host visitors from abroad; you can host an exchange student—after you've gotten settled. If you are worried about forgetting the foreign language you learned abroad, sign up for classes at the adult education center or some other venue. This may also be a way to meet nationals from your overseas post and other returnees who lived there.

* * * * * * *

We realize reentry hasn't come off very well in this chapter, that on the strength of the evidence marshaled here few readers will be inclined to rush out tomorrow and apply for an overseas assignment. While we will try to redress this rather doom-and-gloom attitude in later chapters (and the epilogue), at this juncture we would remind our readers always to consider reentry in the context of the overseas experience that preceded and created it. (See Figure 1.2 for some help here.) You wouldn't have to reenter, after all, if you hadn't gone abroad. But if you hadn't gone abroad, you would never have had the wonderful adventures and experiences that you now sometimes long for, never have met the people you now miss, and never have learned those invaluable lessons about yourself and the world that have changed both you and home forever.

Figure 1.2
Rewards of the Expatriate Experience

Overwhelmed and maybe depressed by reentry, returnees often forget all the ways their overseas sojourn changed them for the better. Herein is a reminder, for those days when you wonder whatever possessed you to go abroad.

1. You learned about another culture and another part of the world.
2. You may now speak a new language, which will be useful in your career or in school.
3. You made some wonderful friends.
4. You are less ethnocentric; you see both yourself and the world more clearly.
5. You are more independent, self-reliant, and self-confident.
6. You can think more creatively or more originally.
7. You are more flexible and may be slower to pass judgment.
8. You know your own culture better than those who never left.

2

The Stages of Reentry

*Even though I'd lived in the same metropolitan area and
country before, this was like moving into a new world, and I
had to start from scratch. I never realized that in returning
home I would not be* instantly *home.*

—Returning spouse

In chapter 1 we described some of the most common problems returnees face during reentry and offered suggestions for coping. In
this chapter our topic is not so much the specific problems returnees confront but the actual process of readjustment, that series of
distinct stages—from departure or leave-taking on through readjustment—which most people report going through. The various
issues described earlier figure prominently in this process, of course,
especially in the reverse culture shock stage, but the experience of
reentry is more than just confronting and solving a laundry list of
problems.

The content of reentry, the actual problems one faces, will be
different for every returnee, but the experience itself does seem to
unfold according to a predictable pattern. For most people this
pattern consists of four stages, each marked by characteristic feelings and behaviors. The length and intensity of each stage will be

different for everyone, but the sequence seems to be consistent. These stages, discussed below, are as follows:

1. Leave-taking and departure
2. The honeymoon
3. Reverse culture shock
4. Readjustment

While reentry is a unique phenomenon in many ways, at its core it is a type of transition and therefore partakes of some of the familiar features of all transitions. The stages listed above, for example, are similar to the three classic steps of any transition: (1) an ending, separation, or disengagement phase; (2) an interim, unstable period; and (3) a beginning, reintegration phase. For our purposes, we have divided the middle, or interim, period into two phases: the initial honeymoon stage and the stage of reverse culture shock.

Realizing that reentry is just another kind of transition can be useful. For one thing it takes some of the mystery out of the experience, for while many returnees may never have been through reentry before, we have all been through transitions of one kind or another and are thus to some extent in familiar territory.

Writing of culture shock, Janet Bennett has observed that it is

> in itself only a subcategory of transition experiences. All such experiences involve loss and change...[and] the reaction to loss and change is frequently "shocking" in terms of grief, disorientation, and the necessity for adjustment.
>
> [In short] we each have some previous experience with the elements of culture shock. Perhaps we have not experienced all the elements, perhaps not in the same form, but nevertheless the similarities may provide us with confidence that we are not entirely without resources. (1977, 92–93)

Another lesson returnees need to recall from previous experience is that transitions by their very nature tend to unfold over time; that is, they are not usually abrupt (though they can be), and you can therefore expect to be "going through" reentry for a considerable period. The problem for many returnees is that while they can readily imagine that moving abroad and adjusting to a foreign culture might be a transition, they see coming home as just a matter of arriving at a certain place on a certain day. They can't fathom, in other words, that coming home is something that will also unfold over time. "When you come back," one observer has noted, "you are supposed to be 'home' and there is great pressure to be completely settled right away. You don't realize that coming back requires a period of adjustment too."

Knowing that these stages are coming and being able to anticipate them, as well as knowing what typically characterizes each stage, can make the reentry experience much less traumatic and unsettling.

Leave-Taking and Departure

In the strictest sense reentry doesn't actually occur until you arrive home. But emotionally and psychologically, it begins several months earlier. A time comes when you start thinking more about the next phase than the current one, when most of your time and effort are spent in preparing to leave the expat culture rather than in adjusting to and living in it. You begin to think about people you want to say good-bye to and wonder how you're going to do that, about places you want to go to and things you want to do before you leave this country, perhaps forever. You may want to find new jobs for household help and dispose of furniture. You may have a pet to arrange for and a car to ship home or sell. You should also be helping your children to think and plan in the same way.

You may feel, incidentally, that saying good-bye just happens naturally, that it isn't something that needs your conscious attention. But because other people are involved, the people you want to say good-bye to, some forethought and coordination may be necessary—if not for you, then perhaps for your children. Without some planning, you may miss the chance to say good-bye to people who are out of town the week you are leaving, or your good-byes may end up being rushed and unsatisfying. What you wanted was to have a certain couple over for a quiet dinner, and instead you had to settle for dropping in on the husband at the office, where he was preoccupied, and calling his wife on the phone. Or your leave-taking might be so haphazard that you forget to say good-bye to certain people altogether. A botched departure can be very demoralizing and a source of considerable regret once you get home. "If the full ritual of leave-taking is not allowed," H. Becker and A. L. Strauss have written, "the [returnee] may not pass fully into his/her new status" (1956, 253).

48

There is also a great deal of anticipation and excitement built up during this phase, plans for what you are going to do when you get back and intimations of how you will feel being home again. You visualize certain encounters and rehearse expected conversations. You begin to look forward to a lot of things you haven't permitted yourself to think about since you have been abroad. Your expectations become more concrete and specific, though not necessarily more realistic. You may also find yourself more critical of your host country than you have been before, in part because you are beginning to disengage from it and identify more closely with home.

Emotionally, this is a bittersweet time. You are looking forward to going home and seeing family and friends again, but you are sad at the prospect of leaving your overseas life and friends behind. Because of your ambivalence, you may have significant mood swings during the last few weeks before departure, what might be called pretransition jitters. One moment you're enthusiastic about starting the next chapter of your life, and the next moment you're overcome with apprehension about the considerable uncertainty that lies ahead. You feel that everything should be much clearer—either we're doing the right thing or we're not—but it can't be clear, of course, for no one knows the future. The same kind of ambivalence, incidentally, is typical of most major life changes, such as getting married, taking a new job, or the imminent birth of a first child.

There may also be some tension in the family during this stage. If the employee's spouse and children have come to enjoy their life abroad, they may not be keen to leave. While they probably understand the necessity of leaving, children and the so-called "trailing spouse" often feel powerless in this situation and may be resentful. The employee may not want to leave either, of course, or have any choice in the matter, but he or she is still seen as the cause of the problem (more so than the real cause, the employer). This can make for a complicated family dynamic, with the employee feeling sad about leaving and guilty about causing so much family anguish, and the spouse and children feeling angry (at having to leave) and guilty (because it isn't entirely the employee's fault).

49

The Honeymoon

For nearly everyone the first week or two after arriving home are close to perfect, very much what you imagined coming home would be like. Everyone is glad to see you and you are happy to see them. Typically you spend this time traveling and visiting old friends and family members. You are a guest wherever you go—not to mention a minor celebrity. You create a sensation whenever you drive into someone's yard, walk into a room, or say hello into the telephone. Wherever you are, you are the undisputed center of attention. People are interested in your stories and want to see some of your videos or slides (or are too polite to act otherwise). Fortunately, you tend not to stay in any one place long enough for people to get over the novelty of seeing you again or for you to start feeling restless. Your contact with most people and most places is so fleeting and charged that you also don't notice (or choose to ignore) any changes that might have taken place, in you and in others. And you haven't had time yet, in all the excitement of being back, to think about—much less miss—your life and friends overseas.

This is also the time when you do all the things you've missed doing while you were gone: You go to that favorite restaurant and have your favorite dish; you have a picnic in the park you love; you go to the bookshop, fabric shop, garden center, or computer shop you've missed and stay for hours just looking; you drink all you want of a favorite drink and eat all the strawberry ice cream or sushi or fish and chips you can stand; you can't get enough of golfing at your favorite course or working in your garden. "When asked what I wanted for my first dinner," Marcia Miller writes, "I unhesitatingly answered, 'A simple salad, plenty of lettuce.' What a pleasure! In one year, I had not tasted one piece of lettuce, had not had one salad or one piece of raw vegetable except for some tomatoes at the end of my stay" (13).

Everyone is solicitous during this stage, wondering how to be of help, and no one expects or demands very much of you either, nothing more than that you relax and enjoy being back home. If people have issues or problems they want to talk with you about, responsibilities they want you to start sharing, important decisions they want you to make, or old axes they want to grind, they hold off during this period, recognizing that you need time to visit with people, to settle in and get your bearings, to take care of pressing practical matters. Virtually the only responsibilities you have during this stage are to show up on time and clean your plate.

Your daily life during this stage will probably remind you of a vacation or home leave. Because you may not have settled into

50

any place yet, you haven't had to confront many of the realities of home, certainly not in the way you will when you eventually move into your house or flat and start living in your neighborhood. You have few real responsibilities and no important decisions to make. Very few of the myriad tasks that await the homecomer have to be performed—or thought about—at this point. Your life is in effect on hold until such time as you choose (or are obliged) to take it up again.

You are not particularly objective about your home country during this stage, being predisposed to see everything in a positive light and passing over anything that doesn't meet your sunny expectations. You don't see home so much for what it is but for what you need it to be. You expect and very much want to be happy during this period, and so you manage to be so. At some level you may sense that this idyll can't quite be real, but you keep any intimations of a less pleasant reality at some considerable distance until you feel strong enough to deal with them.

Reverse Culture Shock

If all this sounds too good to last, rest assured that it is. Depending on circumstances, the honeymoon stage of readjustment may last anywhere from a week or two to as long as a month and may not be the same for all family members. It will also not end abruptly. But gradually the vacationlike unreality of the first part of readjustment will start to fade and be replaced by the appearance of the various syndromes and dynamics discussed in chapter 1 and the rest of this book.

Reverse culture shock normally sets in when you have finished your rounds of visits with family and close friends and the time has come to settle down and start your new life back home. By now your novelty value has started to wear off; people are used to your being back, though you are far from used to it. Moreover,

51

people expect you to have settled in now and assume that you are happy being among family and friends again. They don't ask you how you're doing during this stage—they think they know—and more or less leave you to your own devices. At a time when you may be suffering the most, everyone assumes you're fine.

Judgments

During the honeymoon stage, it seemed that nothing about home or your compatriots could upset you. During this stage, nothing about either of them pleases you. Suddenly, the things you don't like about home stand out with great clarity, while anything you might like barely registers. Everything about your experience abroad is remembered as being perfect—and whatever wasn't perfect isn't remembered. Your mood is such that you can ride the subway and be disgusted by the filth, without remembering how much you hated having to take the fume-spewing taxis in Bangkok because that poor excuse for a city had no subway system. Or you can be appalled at how much food is wasted at a dinner party and neglect to notice how many helpings of dessert you're eating because these are the first decent strawberries you've had in more than two years.

If you've always thought of yourself as tolerant, you may be shocked at how judgmental you have suddenly become. You can't seem to stop reacting to things or noticing and criticizing the various ways that home, including the people, just doesn't measure up. For all intents and purposes, you appear to have lost the ability to be objective, and patient. What's worse is that in your more lucid moments you realize that many of the things you object to are in fact quite trivial and not really worthy of any notice, positive or negative. Not only are you upset, you realize, you are upset about things that don't matter. Don't be surprised, incidentally, if family and friends occasionally find you insufferable during this period as well.

52

As noted earlier, it is normal for returnees to compare home unfavorably with abroad, but this judgmental streak we are speaking of here is of a different breed. It's one thing, after all, to find home lacking in some respects, but it is quite another to be *determined* that home will not measure up to Madrid or Sydney. At the culture shock stage of reentry, however, this rather vehement rejection of home is understandable, for it is not really home that is the problem here but your unsettled emotional state. Notice, for instance, how irrational your responses are; in some cases, the stimulus you react to may be quite insignificant and the degree of your reaction out of proportion to the specific behavior or circumstance you find offensive. This mismatch between stimulus and response is a strong indication that you are reacting not so much to home itself, to the particular triggering events, but to the general insecurity and unhappiness you feel at times during reentry. Sojourners "return more critical of their own society," Gary Weaver has written. "While overseas, they necessarily became more tolerant of other points of view...and had to open their minds to new ways of perceiving reality. Interestingly, this great tolerance and open-mindedness is not always extended to those back home" (4).

Being hard on home serves another useful purpose: It allows you to keep home at arm's length, which is often just where you want it during the early weeks of reentry. After all, you still miss abroad very much during this period and are consequently quite ambivalent about home. So it can be a kind of comfort to keep home at a safe distance until you have sorted out your feelings about it. Until you are ready to embrace home, perhaps it's better that its charms elude you.

Life at the Margins

It is during the reverse culture shock phase of reentry that returnees begin to realize how much they changed while they were abroad and to realize as well how those changes now set them apart from their compatriots. As we noted in chapter 1, living abroad, by its very nature, virtually teems with formative, life-changing experiences—intense, vivid, profoundly felt moments which alter forever your feelings about yourself, others, and the world you live in. Inevitably, you shed some of the values, attitudes, and behaviors of your home culture and take on some of those of both the foreign culture and the expatriate subculture within the foreign country. While you do not become an Italian or an Ecuadorian while living in Rome or Quito, neither do you remain entirely a person from your own culture. Upon reentry, then, you are something of a cultural hybrid, viewing and responding to the world around you from the perspective of two different realities, partaking of each but not fully belonging to either. "I don't think I'll ever have a complete sense of belonging here in America," one returnee remembers, "or for that matter, overseas, because I've been split in two, culturally."

You have become what is called a marginal person, functioning more—and better—at the edges of your society rather than at the center, more likely to be an observer of, rather than a participant in, the scene around you. In many ways, it's like being a member of a minority; you can expect many people to see things quite differently from how you see them, to fail to see certain other things altogether, and in general not to feel about or react to things the way you do. You can also expect not to have some of the same values, attitudes, and opinions of people who are in the mainstream and therefore feel that your point of view is not understood. Like other minorities, returnees have to be careful what they say around people, careful not to project their own values and feelings into situations, careful to hang back and take the measure of things, to see the lay of the land before they act. One returning executive notes,

When I left I severed a lot [of relationships] and although it takes time to build up relationships, [they are] something very different now. I don't really fit, not just at work but socially. I tend not to belong.... I kind of sit [observing everything], like I did in England. And when I think about who I can confide in about [how] I am feeling, I just have my wife. I cannot explain my feelings to anyone who hasn't traveled. You know, once you see the other side, [things are not the same].

You discover, largely through trial and considerable error, that you can't entirely trust your instincts anymore. You have to monitor your behavior more closely because, for the first time, many of the things you would do and say naturally, without thinking, will now strike many people as odd or wrong. "Sometimes expatriates mistakenly feel they can really be themselves when they return home," Joyce Sautters Osland has written in *The Adventure of Working Abroad*, "especially if they have consciously repressed themselves in an attempt to conform to another culture. [But] self-monitoring is still a necessity..." (1995, 189).

Discovering your minority status can be unsettling, even frightening; you feel misunderstood, alienated, and alone in your own country. While it is true, of course, that you were also in a decided minority while you were living abroad, and therefore have probably developed many of the skills necessary to function outside the mainstream, it is one thing to be in the minority in a foreign country and quite another to be in the minority back home. Overseas, you are given a lot of leeway precisely because you are an outsider; you aren't expected to always know the right thing to do and say, and you are more readily forgiven when you transgress the local norms. Being overseas "spoils you for the regular life," Bill Barich has written. "When you're moving from country to country in blithe ignorance, you're usually granted the safe passage of an idiot" (1984,

55

ix). But back home, you are not regarded as a foreigner and don't have the same protection expatriates enjoy. And yet, because you are back home, you let your guard down, relying once again on your instincts to keep you out of trouble. It doesn't occur to you, at least not right away, that in fact you're still a foreigner (albeit for different reasons) and that some of the instincts you acquired abroad won't be of much use to you back home.

Doubt

Coming home is turning out to be much more trouble than you expected. Not surprisingly, another feature of this stage of reentry is doubt. Unhappy and disappointed, you naturally begin to question the wisdom of coming home and wonder if you haven't made a mistake. If I dislike so much about my country and am so different from my compatriots, was coming here really such a good idea? You toy with the notion of going back overseas, back "home," though you know that no home exists there for you anymore. And then you start to question yourself because you're having doubts. This doubting can be merely annoying, or it can induce a kind of paralysis, making it impossible for you to act at a time when there are a great many things to be done if you are ever going to feel at home again. If your spouse and children are also having a difficult reentry, your doubts may be all the more intense.

Overwhelmed

Another prominent feature of reverse culture shock is the feeling, perhaps the reality, of having to start over. As described in chapter 1, nothing is really familiar during this period: not the people, not the places, not the way of life. Very little comes naturally to you and virtually nothing is routine. Everything you do—from emptying the garbage to driving to the supermarket to sending a fax—requires your close, conscious attention. The mundane, the minutiae of everyday life, require so much of your energy and time that there is little left for anything else. Indeed, occasionally even some of the minutiae must be neglected or postponed.

This struggle merely to cope, to meet basic survival needs, and the accompanying fear that higher-order needs can't be ignored much longer are what returnees mean when they say they feel overwhelmed by reentry. On the physical/emotional level, being overwhelmed means you are tired much of the time and may have little resistance to flus or colds; you may lose your appetite or indulge in binge eating; you may be irritable and find it hard to concentrate or relax; you may have dramatic mood swings and fitful sleep. To be blunt, you're not much fun to be around.

Writing of the stress of culture shock and, by implication, reverse culture shock, Cornelius Grove has observed that it can

57

> become a problem...when the neurological and endocrine systems are compelled to respond to environmental novelty constantly and over a long period of time. When this happens, the neurological system, and especially the endocrine system, can become debilitated through overstimulation. [This results in] a sharp reduction in the production of white blood cells...which in turns leads to susceptibility to various diseases and/or exacerbation of chronic illness....
>
> Physiologically speaking, culture shock is precisely this state of debilitation, exhaustion, and susceptibility to disease. (1989, 5–6)

Common Reactions

There are a number of common reactions to the various feelings provoked by reverse culture shock, one of the most prominent of which is resistance. You resist adjusting to your home country because you feel that if you adjust to this place, then you will have to stay here. Many returnees feel so alienated and dislike home so much at the time of reentry that the idea of having to live there is unacceptable. Indeed, during this stage of readjustment, as a survival mechanism, you may comfort yourself with the little fiction that you are not really returning home for good but only temporarily. True, there is no other overseas posting on the horizon, but now that you are back and unhappy, you will scurry around to find one. It may be several months or a year, but make no mistake about it—you *are* going back overseas.

Returnees also resist readjusting for another reason; they equate it with a rejection or at least an undermining of the personal and professional growth they experienced while they were abroad. "Each homecomer has tasted the magic fruit of strangeness," Alfred Schuetz has written,

> *be it sweet or bitter. Even amid the overwhelming longing for home there remains the wish to transplant into the old pattern something of the novel goals, of the newly discovered means to realize them, of the skills and experiences acquired abroad.* (370–71)

It's almost as if readjusting would mean that your expatriate experience never happened, that you would revert to the person you were before you went abroad. And you'll be damned if you're going to adjust to a culture you don't like anyway if the price is having to suppress or deny the exciting new person you have become. "I don't want to adjust too well," a returning New Zealander wrote, "and lose my critical awareness."

Escape and withdrawal are two common reactions associated with reverse culture shock. You may avoid seeing people, not accept invitations, and cut back on entertaining. You're unhappy and depressed, after all, so why would anyone want to be around you? You may also sleep or at least stay in bed more than usual as a means of avoiding a sometimes unpleasant reality.

Readjustment

For all the stress and unpleasantness of reentry shock, it is not permanent. You do, in the end, get used to being home and can even bring closure to your expatriate experience. You actually reach a stage when your goal in life is no longer to go overseas again as soon as possible, when you focus on your life as it now is and not on how it used to be. This doesn't mean that you suddenly realize you were wrong about home, that it really is a wonderful place and how could you be so blind. Nor does it mean that you deny or forget the expatriate experience and what it has meant to you. The difference, rather, is that you now have a more balanced view of your own country, and you are able to put both home and the overseas experience into perspective. You start to admit that certain things about home are rather nice and, if the truth be told, certain things about living abroad weren't really all that pleasant. You are able to see both places for what they are and no longer curse the former for not being the latter.

So, just what is it that makes you suddenly so calm and objective? Why do the things that so recently galled you about your home country and your compatriots now seem like peccadilloes? Why are you no longer so protective of your overseas experience or so critical of your homeland?

What has happened is that you have been back in your country long enough to start feeling at home—not in the sense that you regard your country as home just yet or begin to identify with it but in the sense that you begin to feel more comfortable, relaxed, and settled. This transformation starts slowly—usually while you are still in the throes of reverse culture shock—and goes largely unnoticed in the beginning. For many people it begins when you unpack boxes and arrange a few items of furniture. All of a sudden there is a handful of familiar objects in familiar places, some knowns among all the unknowns, and upon this modest foundation you begin to build a few tentative routines. As you feel yourself retaking control of bits and pieces of your life, your self-confidence and self-esteem begin to stir and your outlook on things gradually becomes more positive.

Meanwhile, the world outside the home is beginning to look more familiar as well. A few places have become known to you, automatically putting all the unknown ones into context. You begin to sense where one place is in relation to another, and after a few tries, you can drive to the grocery store, to school, and to work without paying close attention. There are familiar people in familiar places now, too, people you recognize and who recognize you.

Both inside and outside of the home, more routines develop, bringing welcome predictability to more and more aspects of your life. As parts of your life become more predictable, you can begin to take more things for granted, and once you can do *that*, you can begin to relax.

Once you can relax again, some of the emotion around reentry—the anxiety, the doubt, the fear—begins to dissipate. You feel less stress, you aren't so tired or irritable all the time, and you don't feel so overwhelmed. At the same time, you start to become more objective; you are able to step back on occasion and observe yourself and home more clearly. When you start to see home as it really is, there are bound to be things about it you will like (even as there continue to be things you do not). At the same time you will also be in a frame of mind to see your overseas experience more objectively and to recognize what was good and not so good about it.

At this stage you also discover, to your great relief, that you can in fact readjust and still hold on to many of the new values and attitudes you acquired overseas. Readjustment, it turns out, is not an either/or proposition, requiring that you choose one culture or the other with which to identify. "I worried that I might be unable to adjust fully to either culture," Marcia Miller writes,

*and would always feel displaced.... I realized that my imme-
diate job was to place my China experience into perspective,
to integrate it as best I could and get on with my life. Some
people, finding reentry so troublesome, tend to negate their
overseas experience and not use their newly acquired cross-
cultural skills and learning. I refused to treat my entire
Daqing experience as nontransferable. One China-returned
teacher told me, "China is just fading into the twilight for
me." I didn't ever want that to happen.*

*I knew that I had to decipher what was most meaning-
ful in my China experience, transfer what I could, and come
to terms with what I could not.... The tasks of readjustment
and transference [are] formidable and cannot be rushed....
One must give the process time. Be Chinese; be patient.*

*I finally realized that I was truly home when I became
less judgmental and perceived China and America as they
are, as cultural entities, each with an up side and a down
side, both of which I could criticize and laugh at. (22–25)*

As your feelings about home become more balanced, your relations with the people at home start to improve as well. You don't
judge them quite so harshly or quickly or react quite so strongly
to things they say and do. And you actually start to discern in
them qualities you like and admire. A returning missionary child
recalls his reentry:

*I never felt good about anything. I went home every day
wondering if there was another person in the whole world
like me. Finally, in my senior year of high school, I decided
that maybe the problem was within me, and I tried to talk
with people and get to know them and accept them, even if
they didn't believe the way I did. I can say that I actually
did have some good times with a few of my classmates. I
realized that quite possibly some [of them were] pretty
neat.... I then could loosen my grip on Brazil.*

Meanwhile, friends and loved ones, no longer thrown on the defensive by your rigidity, start making room for the new you in their lives. Margaret Pusch has written,

> The returnee cannot risk being excluded, and those at home cannot tolerate living with someone who is no longer predictable. Ultimately, new relationships must be forged, ones based on a new set of mutually acceptable expectations. This process [has been] characterized...as an "explicit renegotiation of what used to be an implicit contract between people who want or need to live with one another in home, community or work settings." The returnee usually has to modify foreign-acquired behavior, but searches for ways to maintain some of the benefits derived from living abroad. There is, over time, some testing of new ideas and behavior with compatriots, inviting their tolerance [and] acceptance. (1988, 3)

So how long, you may be wondering, does all of this take? When can you expect to feel normal again? There's not much hard data here, as you might expect. Some returnees report feeling readjusted after three months, others after six, and still others after a year or eighteen months. Some adjust quickly at work but more slowly in their personal lives; others, vice versa. Nancy Adler found that six months was a common milestone, with returnees "generally accepting their situation and reporting feeling 'average,'" that is, neither emotionally higher nor lower than normal (1986, 201). The consensus on the honeymoon stage seems to be that the real high lasts no more than a few days—in some cases, only a few hours—and is then followed by two or three weeks of higher than normal excitement before reentry shock takes hold. In the end there are so many variables affecting reentry (see Figure 2.1) that it's not possible to lay down a meaningful or reliable timetable.

Figure 2.1
Some Variables Affecting Reentry

While we have tried to describe a kind of generic reentry in these pages, in fact the reentry experience is not the same for any two individuals. Some of the key variables are presented below.

1. Voluntary versus involuntary reentry: involuntary is worse.
2. Expected versus unexpected reentry: unexpected is harder.
3. Age: reentry may be easier for older people who have been through more life transitions.
4. Previous reentry experience: the first time is worse.
5. Length of the overseas stay: the longer the sojourn, the greater the chance for adaptation, hence the harder it may be to leave and come home.
6. Degree of interaction with the overseas culture: the more involved you become in the local culture, the harder it may be to leave it behind.
7. The reentry environment: the more familiar and supportive, the easier the reentry.
8. Amount of interaction with the home culture during the overseas sojourn: the more familiar the returnee is with changes in the home culture/company, the easier the reentry.
9. Degree of difference between the overseas and the home culture: the greater the difference, the harder the reentry.

Nor do the stages of reentry necessarily unfold in a neat, orderly progression. Some of the excitement and joy of the honeymoon phase may suddenly crop up during reentry shock, and you may be well into readjustment when you have a day that feels suspiciously like the rougher moments of reentry. You won't be able to look back and pinpoint the day or the week when you slipped from one phase into the next, though you may very well be able to identify key moments or pivotal experiences. But gradually a feeling of contentment will color more and more of your waking hours, and one day you will catch yourself thinking about home—and it will be the very place you have come to.

"Today as I drove along [highway] 73, I felt near home," Victor Hunter remembers,

> *yes, home. Literally, for this is where I now reside. Emotionally, for I have begun to "live" here. Psychologically, for I feel it is where I want to be. But home will always be defined a little more broadly now. This home can house memories of other times and places without being haunted by them. I need not despise one [home] to enjoy another, and I need not be ashamed of missing one while living in another.*
>
> *There will still be times of sadness and much that I will miss [about London]. But I do not want to miss the present by missing the past or miss the "here" for missing the "there."*
>
> *As I said, this mountain highway felt like home today. The valley ranches nestled up against the mountain forest. As I looked beyond the valley and up the scree to the snow-covered peaks of the high country, I saw that...here too is a good place to walk, to think, to sort things out. There are no London plane trees on this high westward heath, but there are aspen aplenty. Both are beautiful, but it's important not to confuse them or attempt to make them what they are not.* (188–89)

Readjustment is the final phase of reentry, but it should not be understood as the closing of the book on the overseas experience, for in a larger sense, reentry never truly ends. After all, people don't actually get over experiences, especially profound ones; instead they incorporate them into their character and personality and respond to all subsequent experience from the perspective of their new self. So it is that you will continue to hark back to and integrate aspects of your overseas experience into your postexpatriate life, applying insights you may have had, using knowledge or skills you acquired overseas, seeing life and the world through the filter of all that happened to you on foreign shores. "My mind has to create things," Ronald Blythe wrote in *Akenfield*, "and, when they are completed, go on to another venture. But some ventures refuse to be over. I never sleep one night without dreaming of Arabia" (in Wilson 1993, 465).

3

The Return of the Employee

The expatriate will be transformed from an exotic fish in a small pond to an insignificant minnow in the corporate sea.
—Clare Raffael *Times of London*

Challenging as it is, the personal side of coming home is only one dimension of the reentry experience. Most adults, except for non-working spouses and college students, also return to the workplace and must readjust to their jobs. Whether you work in the private sector, for the government, the military, a college or university, or any other kind of organization or institution, the return to work poses its own set of issues quite distinct from those discussed in chapter 1—but which are also the result of numerous unmet expectations and all manner of unexpected adjustments. While these dimensions of reentry are treated separately in this book, returnees don't experience them in such a neat, orderly sequence. Rather, they confront nearly all of the issues simultaneously.

In some ways, the professional side of reentry is similar to the personal side. For one thing, just as home is no longer home in many ways, neither is the company or organization you come back to the same as the one you left. And just as you have changed personally while you were abroad, you are a different person professionally as well. In other ways, however, the return to work is different, especially when it comes to the strategies that can help you have a softer landing. While you are more or less on your own in coping with the personal side of reentry, both you and your employer play equal roles in a successful return to the workplace. Hence, we will be looking at professional reentry from the perspective of both the employee and the organization.

Issues for the Employee

Off to the Provinces

One of the most common—and most serious—complaints of returning expatriates is that their organization doesn't value or at least doesn't make use of their international experience. These employees have developed considerable knowledge of the international side of operations and also have in many cases a unique global perspective on issues central to the company's well-being. They have also developed skills in dealing with global issues and interacting with people from other cultures, may have learned a foreign language, and are likely to have important contacts in one or more foreign countries. Moreover, many of these employees have been deeply stimulated by their expatriate experience and now have a keen interest in the overseas side of the business. They want very much to keep working in the international arena and use the knowledge and skills they have acquired. Under the circumstances, to be put in charge of provincial marketing or suburban sales is something of a disappointment. In a survey of more than 250 multinational corporations, 76 percent of those responding said the single most effective thing a company could do to minimize expatriate turnover would be to give returnees a "chance to use their international experience" (Global Relocation 1999, 43).

"My current position has very little to do with what I learned overseas," a Japanese returnee noted. "What a waste for this company, to spend all the money to send me overseas and then bring me back and not even utilize what I learned while I was there." In a recent study of expatriates, two-thirds of the Japanese and four-fifths of the Americans surveyed felt their company did not value their expatriate experience, and only 39 percent of the Americans reported using that experience in their reentry jobs. "Your own perceived increase in 'value' after an international experience," an American returnee remarked, "is just that—*perceived*. Expatriates should be prepared for the fact that few—precious few—people are interested in their international experience."

These complaints, incidentally, are no less common in so-called global companies, many of which realize more than half their revenues from overseas operations, as they are in companies that may have an international division but a largely domestic focus. One can understand that it might not always be possible to place every returnee in the perfect job, but undervaluing the returnee shows up in many other ways as well. Colleagues aren't especially interested in where you have been or what you have done. There is no formal recognition of your return or official thanks for the great job you did in New York or Taipei. Nor are you asked to brief anyone, to share the lessons you have learned with those people back at headquarters who have responsibility for the international side of the business. Employers who do value an expatriate's international expertise often think that it is only useful or relevant in the field, not back in headquarters (where most of the key decisions affecting the field are typically made) or on the domestic side of operations (which often face stiff competition from some of the very countries on which these unhappy returnees are now experts).

Power Failure

Another common frustration reported by returnees is the loss of responsibility and authority in their new position back home, the phenomenon sometimes referred to as "job shrink." In one study, more than three-fourths of American managers and over half of Finnish managers reported being placed in a lower-level position upon their return than they had overseas (the Japanese clocked in at 43 percent). The economics of posting people abroad is such that most employers cannot afford to support a large group of expatriates, with the result that those few who are sent abroad are typically given much broader responsibility than would any manager at their level back home—as they find out soon enough upon reentry. "Let's say you've just spent three years as general manager of a branch in Tokyo," notes Dan Kendall, in charge of employee benefits for Rohm and Haas. "You get used to the freedom you had to make fairly major decisions, like having the authority to make expenditures of $50,000. The first time you come back to the home office and find you must comply with twenty-two rules and regulations in order to buy a pencil, you're likely to be outraged" (Williams 1986, 32).

Once you have tasted this kind of authority, it is difficult to relinquish it—hard, that is, to go from being the only senior manager in Osaka to one of twenty-six back in Brussels. "A forty-year-old man can be the head of the pharmaceutical division in Indonesia," a Swiss executive observes. "The pay is good and the person assumes lots of responsibilities. Back here, he is just one of hundreds."

Autonomy Blues

In a related complaint, many returnees also report a severe loss of autonomy and independence when they come home. Expatriate managers on the scene aren't normally second-guessed by their superiors back home. It doesn't make sense, for one thing—why go to the expense of fielding expatriates and then micromanage them? And it's often quite impractical because of the time and distance involved. So it is that expatriates get into the habit of making important decisions more or less on their own, without consultation or extensive discussions with higher-ups. Back home, where there are often more layers of management, even routine decisions have to be discussed at numerous meetings and approved at several levels. In the study cited above, nearly half the American managers and exactly half the Japanese managers reported less autonomy in their reentry positions. "One minute [you're] Patton roaring across the desert," a management consultant has observed, "and the next [you're] on Eisenhower's staff where the moves must be made an inch at a time."

Loss of Status

The loss of status upon reentry also means that you probably don't rub elbows with the power brokers very often these days. When you were our man in Riyadh or our woman in Chicago, some very important people passed through your life. They visited you in the field—vice presidents, CEOs, deans, or generals—and they met with you when you came back on home leave. They sent you faxes, e-mail, called you on the phone; and they took your calls, read your faxes, and skimmed your e-mail. They may have called you by your first name and asked you to call them Sara or Hans. They treated you almost as one of them. Now you pass these same people in the hall, assuming you have halls in common, and they don't quite manage to make eye contact.

No Growth

The loss of authority and autonomy characteristic of coming home often leads to a slowing down of your professional growth. Overseas, you were learning something new every day and developing important skills. Work was challenging and stimulating; you were being routinely stretched beyond the limits of your knowledge and abilities. You could almost feel yourself maturing as a professional. Now, back home, you may find that your new position doesn't really challenge you or demand that much of you, in part, perhaps, precisely because you have grown so much in your overseas posting. You feel that professionally you're only just holding your own, or possibly losing ground. "When you are overseas, you know you are in a learning environment," one returnee has remarked. "Everything is exciting. You feel as though you are growing. When you move back [home], you feel as though, 'Here I am at square one.' It's a very depressing situation to be in. You feel you are not growing anymore."

Holding Patterns

For some returnees the problem isn't so much the job they end up with but ending up with no job at all. You are put into a kind of holding pattern, given an office and a desk, perhaps, maybe a title and a secretary, but no real responsibility. In fact, you don't really have a job yet but are given the trappings of one until management can figure out what to do with you. To go from a situation where you were, if anything, overworked to one where you have no real work at all can take some getting used to. "What they don't tell you beforehand," one executive remarked,

> and I don't care how compassionate your company may be, is that they have no idea what they are going to do with you when it comes time to bring you home. When I reminded them that it was time to bring me back, I could sense that they were trying to cope with my return, as though they were saying, "Now what are we going to do with the s.o.b.?"

Out of Sight, Out of Luck

In a way, many of the problems cited above are part of a larger issue: the whole matter of "out of sight, out of mind." Except in the few organizations that do strategic personnel planning and actually map out precise career plans for senior employees, returnees usually have to rely on luck when it comes to a reentry assignment, taking whatever is available that even remotely matches their qualifications and management level. Sometimes nothing is immediately available, and they get the phantom jobs mentioned above.

This isn't because the right vacancies don't open up—jobs that would be a perfect match for someone with the expat's experience—but because expats are often overlooked while they're abroad and not considered for any new position until close to the time they are due to return (or after). For all practical purposes, their careers are on hold until they come back from overseas—in a way, incidentally, that is almost never true of employees at their same level working at headquarters. Employees at headquarters, for example, are routinely considered available for vacancies for which they qualify, but an expatriate who qualifies for that same position is often considered unavailable because he or she is overseas. "International experience is great," one senior executive observed. "Make sure you get it in the international division at headquarters—right down the corridor from the chairman of the board."

For many returnees, being out of sight and out of mind means they have been overlooked for promotions, with their peers or their juniors getting the job they were next in line for at the time they went abroad. In their research Black et al. found that only 11 percent of Americans, 10 percent of Japanese, and 25 percent of Finns were promoted after completing a two-year expat assignment. What is even more stunning, they report that 77 percent of Americans, 43 percent of Japanese, and 54 percent of Finns were actually *demoted* after returning home. As one Finnish expatriate has observed, "When you go overseas, your firm absolutely forgets you in terms of promotions. In fact, my overseas assignment seems more like a punishment, in terms of my career" (1992, 237).

Catching Up

The expat assignment can take its toll on your career in other ways, too. You may find yourself behind the times professionally, having been unable to keep up with developments in your field while you were overseas. There may be new technologies at work that you will need to learn: new software, for example, or new versions of older software.

You may not know some or most of the new players in your department or division, or you may be assigned to a new division altogether. You will need to establish relationships with scores of new people and reestablish relationships with people you haven't seen or worked with for several years. Certain policies and procedures or perhaps the entire focus or vision of the organization or department will have changed in your absence. There may be new products and services, new buzzwords, new rules of conduct. "Our organizational culture was turned upside down," one returnee observed. "We now have a different strategic focus, different 'tools' to get the job done, and different buzzwords to make it happen. I had to learn a whole new corporate language."

In the worst cases, your division may have been abolished while you were away, or the company acquired by or merged with another company. Whatever the changes, in much the same way that home is no longer home anymore, the organization you return to is not the one you left.

Among Friends

Another set of repatriation issues concerns how your colleagues and friends feel about your being back and how you feel about being back among them. To begin with, some of your colleagues and friends may not be around anymore. You were looking forward to working with Alice again—she made working in your division worth all the stress and heartburn—but it turns out Alice has left the company and a stranger now sits at her desk (and wonders who you are). Or perhaps there was a mentor who took you under his wing some years ago, looked out for you, put in a good word at opportune moments, and more or less helped you get where you are today. And now he's gone—has retired, quit or moved, or is no longer in favor or has no clout with the new bosses. To the extent that working with certain key people was what made your department or your job so much fun, so stimulating or rewarding, you will feel the absence of such people as a great disappointment.

The other problem, of course, is that certain other people, of whom your memories are less fond, have not moved on. Maybe you had forgotten about them or hoped they had new positions or, better yet, new employers. In any case you haven't had to deal with them for two or three years, and it has been heaven. But now that you're back, the same issues or the same kinds of friction are still there, as unresolved and unpleasant as ever.

Some of your peers may be threatened by you upon your return. You may be one of only a handful of people with international experience in your organization or your division. You're on a familiar basis with several corporate VPs, deans, or heads of departments. You speak French and wear Italian suits. You pose a particular threat in organizations pushing to become more global, where overseas experience is suddenly the ticket to advancement. "I was shocked," one returnee noted, "at the animosity of [my] coworkers because I had learned to work successfully with the Japanese during my international assignment." For many companies, the focus on becoming more global has only crystallized in the last two or three years, while you were away. All at once that questionable career move of taking an expat assignment has propelled you to the forefront of the company's rising stars, without your having done a thing. While this is nice for you, some of your colleagues may not be so pleased to find you suddenly blocking their career path.

You may also be shocked at the provincialism of some of your colleagues and at how little they know about the international side of operations—and how little they care. "My coworkers ridiculed me," a Japanese returnee recalled, "for carrying and reading *Newsweek* at the office after I had spent four years in the United States. They made me feel like a traitor to my company." In some cases the apparent ignorance and lack of interest on the part of colleagues may be a defense mechanism, a way of meeting the threat you represent by simply dismissing your experience, but in other cases it is quite genuine. Even in the most global-minded of organizations, many employees aren't yet true believers. They say the right things, but their instincts are still domestic; they hold on to the belief that anything of real importance that happens in the organization takes place in the home culture, especially at headquarters. People may think "it's great over there," one returnee recalled,

> but it's over there after all, and that's not as important as what happens in Keokuk, Iowa.... The patterns [may be] breaking down, but historically it's been, "Well, it's nice he's been there and we'll take advantage of it from time to time, but basically the way you're successful is being successful here."

So it is that colleagues won't ask you many questions about what happened "over there" and certainly won't be able to carry on an intelligent conversation about the work you were doing. In the worst cases, they may feel your overseas sojourn, two or three years out of the loop, has lessened what you can offer the organization. You will have to be brought back up to speed.

This professional loneliness is very much like the personal loneliness discussed in chapter 1, with much the same result. Just as not being able to tell friends and loved ones about your life overseas makes you feel they don't know you anymore, not being able to talk about your professional experiences and insights with colleagues makes you feel like an outsider. Indeed, the emotional distance you and your colleagues feel from each other may keep you on the periphery or outside of important business and social networks.

Meanwhile, Back at the House

Readjustment to work may also be complicated by matters on the home front. If your spouse and children are having a difficult reentry, which is more than likely, then much of your time and energy is being diverted in that direction, which may slow down your adjustment at work. Black et al. found a statistical correlation between the successful adjustment of the family and the performance of the employee on the job, creating what they call a "spillover effect in which the productive home situation spills over to work and increases an expatriate's effectiveness." As one employee noted,

> My spouse has had a very difficult time coming home from Europe and living in the suburbs of America. She hates it. Her adjustment difficulty has made my life less than wonderful and my work performance has been less than excellent.

No One to Turn To

Professional reentry, like personal reentry, is a lonely experience. Chances are you are the only person going through it in your organization, unless other expats happen to be returning at the same time. And most of the people around you won't know what reentry is, much less that it can be difficult. While there may be people whose job it is to help you, usually members of the human resources division, in most cases these people have not been overseas. Indeed, in many companies expats, up to now the responsibility of international human resources, are turned over to domestic HR when they return home. This doesn't mean you're suddenly put in the hands of incompetent, unfeeling people—on the contrary, they are usually sensitive and caring professionals—but it often means the people looking out for you have never been through what you are going through and won't always be able to anticipate your needs or understand what you are feeling. Typically, these people are relocation specialists, most of whose experience is with domestic relocation. While their expertise will come in handy, domestic relocation is not reentry. One returnee explains,

> It would have helped at least to have personnel with some understanding of the experience of repatriation. Most of these people have no appreciation of what needs to be done in coming home. Since we had lived internationally and moved back one time before, we knew what to expect and basically had to manage it ourselves.

In any case, the human resources staff are only responsible for the practical side of reentry, the nuts and bolts. They can't do anything about the emotional/psychological side, the fact that you have lost your autonomy and authority or are stuck in a job where you never write, read, or say the word *international*.

Your colleagues won't be much help either, even your best friends. They may be concerned and well intentioned, but they won't understand the issues you face. They may even assume that you're happy to be back at headquarters and not still in exile in some professional backwater halfway around the world. Accordingly, they are going to be a little surprised that you seem to be struggling or that on occasion you seem down or genuinely depressed. It's bad enough that you can't turn to these people for understanding and support, but it's worse when their reactions make you wonder if there's something wrong with you.

Taking the Initiative

The general lack of understanding about reentry on the part of management and others poses another problem for the returnee: if you want to get the kind of help and attention you need during readjustment, personally and professionally, you have to take the initiative. Chances are that colleagues and managers have not anticipated your needs and put systems and programs in place to help you, so you may have to be aggressive, approach people— often repeatedly—and ask them to do things for you. "My husband's company left him dangling in the wind," a returning spouse reports. "No one in the company volunteered anything. He had to initiate everything." If you're not naturally an aggressive person, this may be difficult and frustrating. Moreover, you may run the risk of getting a reputation as a complainer and have to suffer the indignity of watching people in human resources look the other way whenever they see you coming.

Issues for the Organization

The professional side of reentry poses almost as many issues as the personal side. Taken together, which is exactly how they're experienced, these two dimensions of coming home add up to a sizable dose of disappointment, frustration, and in many cases, genuine unhappiness. It is no wonder that fully one-quarter of returnees leave their original company within one year of repatriation and, according to one study, 40 percent leave after two years. Black et al. reported an even more alarming finding: 74 percent of American expatriates "did not expect to be working for the same company one year later, and 79 percent felt that the demand for their international skills was high and that they could find good jobs in other firms" (263).

Assuming most employers want to keep their competent and valuable returnees when they come back, it behooves employers to address the whole matter of reentry and provide a softer landing for returnees. Nor should turnover be the only concern here. Those employees who stay with the organization, who are after all the majority, aren't going to be very effective if they are frustrated and bitter because of a botched reentry.

A Lost Investment

Actually, the stakes here are higher than they might appear at first glance. While it's a given that most employers regret losing valuable employees, to lose an expatriate upon reentry is an especially costly proposition. For the typical global corporation, total expat compensation (counting allowances, cost differentials, and perks) is two and one-half times what that employee would cost the organization back home. For an American corporate executive, for example, with a spouse and two children, the average cost for a three-year overseas tour is between half and three-quarters of a million dollars. When another organization picks up this employee, it is simply helping itself to your investment. If the company that lures your employee away is one of your competitors, your loss is just that much greater.

In some cases, incidentally, you will lose this employee even before he or she becomes a returnee. Many expats, appalled at the slim professional pickings they know await them back home, jump ship and stay on overseas, working for another company. While some expats no doubt prolong the overseas idyll no matter what awaits them back home, for others the certainty of a decent reentry job might be all it would take to keep them in the fold.

Other People Do Notice

But the costs don't end here. Another price employers often pay for unhappy returnees is a marked company-wide cooling off of interest in expatriate assignments. Employees the company is trying to persuade to accept an overseas assignment are not going to be encouraged by what they see happening to people who come home. If they have any doubts at all about going abroad (and for most employees the decision to move abroad is fraught with uncertainties), they're likely to have a few more after a round of drinks with the latest returnee. Given the fact that finding expat candidates is already the single biggest relocation challenge facing most multinational companies, this is not good news for international HR. All of this is especially true, of course, if the returnees' careers appear to have suffered as a result of going abroad. In one survey of two hundred executives, career impact was listed as the number one concern in deciding whether to take an overseas assignment (far ahead of the assignment location and economic considerations). "Faster than anything else," one corporate executive has remarked,

> *poor reintegration...gives expatriate experience a bad reputation. You won't win [with other employees] if they see that the last person who came back was worse off than when he left. Every time there is a casualty, it gets magnified more than a hundredfold. Like everything in life, everybody knows about the casualty.*

Indeed, disgruntled returnees can damage a company's reputation across the board, not just with potential expatriates, for how they are treated is inevitably seen by other employees as an indication of how well a company takes care of all of its workers.

Once Was Enough

Even in those cases where the employee does not leave the organization, an unhappy repatriation can kill any interest that person might have had in one day taking another overseas posting. Given that this is precisely the kind of person an employer would want to send overseas again—someone who has proven he or she can handle an expat assignment—the loss is that much greater. Moreover, in organizations that do long-term personnel planning, successive overseas assignments in two or three geographic regions are a common way of grooming rising stars for senior management positions. If these stars have troublesome reentries, their interest in going out again may fizzle. So much for the money spent on fast-trackers and the company's carefully crafted succession plan.

Effect on the Sojourn

Perhaps the most important—and certainly the least appreciated—reason to pay attention to reentry is the effect that not having to worry about the return has on an expatriate's performance *while he or she is still overseas*. Many returnees have noted that knowing what their reentry position was going to be, not having to worry about the future correlated with improved performance on the job. In other words, some kind of repatriation program not only ensures the smooth return of the employee but may also ensure a productive sojourn as well.

Alas, recent research shows that very few organizations do this kind of career planning. One study found that two-thirds of expatriates from three different countries did not know what their reentry jobs would be before they returned home.

What the Organization Can Do

Career Planning

If what we have written above suggests anything, clearly it is the need for employers to do more career planning for expatriates. No other single step will strike at the heart of more of the problems of professional reentry, most of which, after all, are job-related disappointments. If there are no surprises upon reentry, if the expatriate knows what job he or she is going to have, at what level, in which division, under whom, supervising whom, and so on—in other words, if the returnee's job expectations are realistic—much of the pain of reentry is automatically eliminated.

And the sooner this career plan is designed, the better. Ideally, it is worked out before the employee goes overseas. Indeed, if the organization has "done its homework," the decision to send the employee abroad will not be a spontaneous act but an integral part of an overall strategy which charts the employee's career for the next ten to fifteen years or more. In this context the expatriate assignment is merely the preparation for the return assignment, which in turn is the preparation for the next step, culminating in the position from which he or she retires or joins the executive ranks. In such a scheme, incidentally, repatriation planning is not done to ease the burden of reentry (though it will have that effect) but simply as a matter of course.

Though not designed specifically to do so, this kind of planning is almost guaranteed to mitigate at least two of the most serious complaints of returnees: they will have a real job upon reentry, and the position is likely to have at least as much responsibility as the overseas job, since each step in the career plan builds upon the previous one. As for a third key concern of many returnees—landing a job that uses one's international experience—career planning, by definition, greatly increases the chances of this happening as well. But there are no guarantees. In some cases even with the best career planning, there just aren't any timely vacancies requiring overseas experience, or there may be vacancies but too many candidates for the positions that are available.

In many cases employees are sent overseas because of an immediate operational need or to "put out a fire." As a rule, this kind of assignment does not lend itself to career planning and may leave returning expatriates out of luck. Nevertheless, organizations that do a good deal of this kind of posting could put systems in place to make reentry easier on their employees. Beyond that, they should try to see those operational needs in advance, thereby making overseas posting and reentry less arbitrary and abrupt.

Repat Agreements

While career planning is the single most important thing employers can do to ease the pain of reentry, it will not be possible in all organizations. Indeed, one study of corporate America found that only 23 percent of overseas assignments were made as a result of manpower planning versus 67 percent made in response to an immediate operating need. And in those organizations where career planning is the norm, there are always unforeseen developments that will force changes in the best-laid career plans. For organizations that don't do career planning, as well as for those that do, a number of other measures can be taken to soften the blow of reentry.

One possibility, in effect the next best thing to career planning, is a repatriation agreement in which the company promises the employee will be placed in a mutually acceptable job upon reentry. There may be no specifics at this point—no mention of a particular job or division, no promise of a promotion or a certain salary—but at least the organization has gone on record as being concerned about reentry and has committed itself to the employee's best interests upon his or her return. "We improved acceptance of overseas assignments by about 20 to 25 percent," an employee relations manager at one multinational company observed in describing one effect of using repatriation agreements. A Westinghouse employee who signed such an agreement before going to Puerto Rico agrees: "It has absolutely alleviated possible career anxieties."

Daniel Kendall, personnel director for Rohm and Haas, observes,

A contract does three very valuable things: (a) it keeps the employee thinking about his return date; (b) it eliminates

the anxiety the expatriate feels about what position, and under what circumstances, he or she will return—particularly as the return gets nearer; (c) it keeps company management back home focused on the return date and forces human resource planning.

Managements...tend to not like the idea of a contract of employment. One hears that a contract "connotes lack of trust," "limits flexibility," and "sounds too much like a union situation." There is almost unquestionable evidence, however, that industry, in order to attract the best people to work abroad, must move in [that] direction. (1981, 21–25)

Expats as Senior Managers

Another move that can make reentry a happier experience for all concerned is to place more former expatriates in senior management positions. While previous expatriate experience will not be the only, or the primary, reason for promoting someone to a senior management position, it is an increasingly important qualification in the era of globalization—and a godsend for returnees. Senior managers who have themselves been expatriates implicitly understand the value of international experience and may go to greater lengths to see that returnees are placed in jobs that use their expertise. Moreover, former expatriates understand the trials of reentry and are likely to be proactive in meeting returnees' needs. In one survey, only 29 percent of American returnees were working for supervisors who had international experience.

Meet My Mentor

Another proactive approach to reentry is to assign a home-based sponsor or mentor to each expatriate. Typically, this person plays a number of roles, many of which address some of the reentry problems described earlier. In general the mentor looks out for the expatriate's interests while he or she is abroad and serves as a conduit of communication between headquarters and the expat on the one hand and between the expat and headquarters on the other. In the latter role, the mentor tries to keep headquarters from forgetting about the expatriate, to keep his or her name in front of people, and to keep senior management abreast of how "our man in Kraków" is doing—in short, to fight off the out-of-sight, out-of-mind syndrome.

In his or her other role, the mentor does just the reverse, keeping the expatriate up to date on what's happening at headquarters: the latest reorganization, new products and procedures, new technologies, new directions, new players. In this capacity the mentor also keeps an eye out for upcoming vacancies the expat ought to be considered for and prods management to put the expat's name in the "hopper" though he or she is abroad. Ideally, the mentor also visits the employee overseas and spends time with the expat when he or she is on home leave. Many mentors feel their job is over once the expat is back on home soil, but the best ones track their charges for several months after they have returned to make sure they have landed on their feet.

Staying in the Loop

Communication between headquarters and the field, one of the key tasks of the mentor (and lack of it one of the chief complaints of expats), can be addressed in other ways, all for the greater good of enabling returnees to set realistic expectations about home and creating what we might call the no-surprises reentry. A newsletter for expats—it only has to be one page—lets them follow what is happening at headquarters and gives them advance warning that their division has been abolished or sold. Some organizations update expats with videotapes, showing changes back home, including personal hellos from colleagues and friends. Employers should also advertise vacancies worldwide and in a timely manner so that going abroad doesn't have to mean your career is on hold until

---

Figure 3.1
What Returnees Offer Their Organization

Anyone who has been posted abroad comes home with some old skills greatly enhanced and some skills that are new to the organization. Management should highlight these skills and take advantage of them.

1. The returnee may have invaluable knowledge of certain regions, countries, or markets with which the company or organization does business or competes.
2. The returnee brings a different, perhaps unique, perspective to issues, discussions, and problem solving.
3. The returnee is likely to be more flexible in dealing with others and more open to new ideas, more likely to try something that hasn't been tried before.
4. The returnee has increased tolerance for different ideas, behaviors, and opinions and, hence, an increased ability to work with or manage a culturally or ethnically diverse workforce.
5. The returnee is more able to compromise, to be more humble and less rigid.
6. The returnee understands the home culture better, can step outside it and observe objectively how it influences decisions and other organizational behavior.
7. The returnee has more self-confidence, having survived and prospered in a challenging environment.
8. The returnee is a good risk for another overseas assignment.

87

---

you return. Home leave, of course, is another way to keep employees in touch, as are field visits from headquarters staff. Some organizations take home leave one step further and give employees short-term assignments at headquarters to keep their profile high and to keep them current on developments in the home country.

Figure 3.2

Recommended Content for a Repatriation Workshop

A good repatriation seminar is designed to address the key issues of reentry. At a minimum, the following topics should be addressed:

1. What did you like about being overseas and what will you miss the most?
2. Who are you now? How has the overseas experience changed you? What new skills, knowledge, attitudes have you acquired?
3. How has home changed? What the country is like now: an update on economic, political, social, and cultural developments since you left.
4. What are common problems of readjustment?
5. How can you cope with the problems of readjustment? What resources can you turn to?
6. What is your financial situation? What are your options?
7. How can you use your expertise in your new job?
8. What issues are your spouse and children facing? What can you do about these?
9. What is your action plan? What three things are you going to do as a result of this seminar? What specific steps can you take to make your reentry or that of your family less stressful?

Valuing the Expatriate Experience

Even with mentors, career planning, and repatriation agreements, some returnees are not going to get jobs that use their international experience. But this doesn't have to mean that the organization devalues such experience or that it must necessarily go to waste. To begin with every returnee, whether he or she is destined to cover Indonesia or northern Idaho, should get some kind of an

---

Figure 3.3
What Others Can Do

Returnees have to shoulder most of the burdens of reentry themselves. But managers and colleagues can help by being sympathetic and by not making the situation worse than it already is.

1. Show interest. You can listen to the stories returnees have to tell, ask questions (should the need arise), and then pay attention to the answers.

2. Provide opportunities for returnees to use their new skills and knowledge. Invite them to attend selected meetings or to make a presentation to certain committees or divisions. Make an effort to consult with returnees on issues where their overseas experience or perspective might be useful. This helps the company, of course, and also makes returnees feel their knowledge is valued.

3. Avoid overreacting when returnees criticize the organization. Returnees often feel frustrated and take out their frustration, in some cases, on their employer and colleagues. Sometimes they just need to let off steam, and you can help by being a sounding board. If the criticisms are unjust or unfair, this can be gently pointed out when the returnee has calmed down.

4. Try not to feel threatened or offended if returnees make unflattering comparisons between colleagues back home and those overseas. They are disappointed and unhappy about a lot of things and may take it out on you. Given half a chance, they will probably apologize later.

5. Be patient and do not expect returnees to fit back in and be happy right away. Avoid making judgments the first few weeks; a lot of the behaviors will drop away in due time.

Figure 3.3 (cont.)

6. Check in from time to time during the first few months and ask the returnee how everything is going. He or she will be thrilled that somebody asked, that somebody else realizes reentry can be difficult.

---

official welcome home, an event designed specifically to thank this person for the work done away from headquarters and the contribution made to the organization. Such an event also reintroduces the employee to the organization and allows him or her to meet key new players. Bruce La Brack has said of this event:

[Although] it is often overlooked, or handled so casually that it loses its potential as a powerful ritual of reintegration, the "welcome back" can be celebrated in such a way that it becomes a significant marker for the company and individual. As a rite of passage, the welcome of returnees home has roots in tribal societies, [and] probably goes back millennia, as they seek to find a place for their wandering kinsmen.

Veteran returnees understand and value this recognition and may be willing to take charge to insure that recently returned company members are properly acknowledged and their achievements noted. Formal or informal, it signals to others that company management really values the sacrifices and cross-cultural knowledge and skills an overseas assignment [represents]. Welcoming back isn't a frill, but an essential public ceremony to validate the returnee and reaffirm the organization's commitment to those it sends abroad. (1993, 2)

In a Windham International survey of global relocation, 59 percent of respondents indicated that "greater recognition" after an assignment would help reduce expat turnover.

Returnees should also be asked to brief key managers and executives on what they learned overseas. Such a briefing could include an overview of the latest developments in their part of the world and the insights they have gained in their two years abroad—insights into working in the international arena and on how the organization is perceived from the overseas side of operations. In addition to oral briefings with key people, returnees could also be asked to write up their observations in a report that is distributed to appropriate employees.

Another way returnees can use their expertise is by serving as mentors to the latest batch of expatriates. In addition, they should be used in orientation workshops for those going abroad and briefings for headquarters staff headed overseas on business trips. They should also be invited to serve on task forces and committees that have any kind of international focus (whether in their department or technical area or not). In general their opinions should be sought whenever decisions concerning international operations are being made, including policy decisions that will affect all employees in the organization. Figure 3.1 on page 87 describes what the returnee offers the organization.

Reentry Orientation

Another major component of a smooth reentry is some kind of readjustment orientation and training for employees and their families (see Figure 3.2, page 88, for suggested content). This workshop should touch upon all of the major issues of reentry, personal and work-related, and help guide the employee, spouse, and children through the experience. Ideally, it would be held for a group of returnees who could comfort each other by swapping stories. The timing of this event can vary, from several months before departure from abroad to just before departure to just after reentry or a few weeks after reentry. Some organizations cover reentry in the expat orientation given before the employee goes into the field. There is probably no ideal time for this event. If the company holds it too soon, the expats will wonder what is being talked about; if it is held too late, they will wonder why it took so long to get around to it. The best solution is probably to hold the workshop in two phases: the first phase a week or two before the expat and family leave for home, and the second phase three weeks to a month after reentry.

A related suggestion here is to conduct reentry support workshops for the people who will be working with the returnee. To the extent that colleagues, the boss, and subordinates understand what the returnee is going through, they can work more smoothly with the returnee (see Figure 3.3, pages 89–90). At the same time it helps the returnee to know that other people understand what it's like to come home. Such a workshop, by the way, should include human resources staff, who may not be colleagues of the returnee but with whom the returnee will have significant interaction. In the best of all possible worlds, some of the human resources staff would be returnees themselves.

Time Off

Many returnees just don't have enough time to do all of the things coming home requires, the things that can't wait. Employers would be wise to give returnees some time off before expecting them to report to work. This not only takes the pressure off, it also increases the chances that when returnees do report to work, they will be able to keep their minds on the job. If the employee has used up his or her vacation time, which often happens en route from overseas, consider offering an advance on leave or leave without pay. In the same vein, allow employees to temporarily come and go as they need to, so long as they work the number of hours required. "Recently returned expatriates...need a grace period at work," Joyce Osland has written, "[including] lower performance expectations, until they are settled in and get their feet on the ground. At a bare minimum, [they] should be kicked out of the office exactly at closing time until they get their family settled" (219).

Financial Help

The employer can also help the returnee deal with the financial shock of reentry. To begin with the company or organization should offer financial counseling to employees before they depart on their overseas assignment. The employee should be told what degree of salary shrink to expect upon reentry and be given an estimate of typical readjustment expenses, including any unanticipated income taxes. Ideally, the employee should be encouraged to start saving for the return before leaving the home country. Many organizations pay a monthly expat bonus, which is typically built into the regular paycheck—and is spent right along with it. Employers might consider holding a few months of this money in a "readjustment account," which the expat can't touch until he or she comes home.

For many returnees, especially Americans, the most daunting expense they face is buying a new house. Whenever possible, employees should be encouraged not to sell their home when they go overseas, and the organization should do what it can to support this decision. Coming up with a down payment and closing costs for a new house puts a severe strain on a returnee's finances at a time when there are already an extraordinary number of other expenses. Moreover, with all of the other challenges the returnee faces, the stress of house hunting—and the pressure, from within and without, to find something quickly—is just one more trauma the returnee can do without. In some cases employers act as rental agents for expats or retain the services of a property management company. Or the expat can hire such a company directly.

93

For some expats, it may not be practical or possible to keep their home or flat. In that case, when they return, the organization might be able to offer a low-interest housing loan and some kind of temporary living arrangement. In these instances, it is particularly important to give the employee plenty of time to settle in and maximum flexibility in work hours; for house or flat hunting is a time-consuming business. Organizations can also offer other financial help, including an interim housing allowance, free rental car, low-interest car loans, tax counseling, and financial planning upon reentry.

What's Good for the Family...

How well the family adjusts, as noted earlier, affects how well the employee performs on the job. Employers would do well, then, to pay attention to the return of the family—as the decent thing to do, of course, but also for the good of the company. Family members should be included in any kind of repatriation workshop offered by the employer, and an attempt should be made to introduce returning spouses to other spouses who have been through reentry. Returning children should likewise be introduced to the children of other returnees who have gone or are going through reentry. Some organizations have repatriation committees made up of returned spouses who sponsor events (picnics, camping trips) for the latest returnees and their families. Spouses and older children should be debriefed about their overseas and reentry experiences and used as resources in both predeparture and reentry orientations for new families moving abroad. Career counseling and job-hunting support are two other areas where spouses often need assistance, and psychological counseling for spouse and children is another common need.

A relocation kit is a useful item for returning families, including such items as area maps; change of address labels; the names and phone numbers of car rental agencies, reliable real estate agents, and recommended baby-sitters; information on managing pets and registering a car; and other useful addresses and phone numbers.

What the Employee Can Do

While you may be lucky enough to work for an organization that understands the difficulties of reentry and has addressed them, the statistics are not on your side. Consider these findings (from several studies):

- 89 percent of respondents said they received no repatriation training from their organization.
- 95 percent of American companies gave less than six months' notice of return.
- 59 percent of Finnish expats reported that their firm's repatriation processes were unclear.
- 80 percent reported their companies did not value international experience.
- 69 percent of expatriates did not have mentors while they were serving abroad.

For the time being, until more employers become proactive regarding reentry issues, you should assume that you will be left to your own devices upon your return.

Planting Seeds

So where do you start? If you are still at home when you read this and are about to be posted overseas, you will want to talk with management about their reentry process and your reentry position. If management draws a blank, you can at least suggest that they start thinking about how to bring people home (in particular, you). If you can, try to draw up some kind of repatriation agreement that at least commits management to thinking about you from time to time while you are gone. And try to link up with a mentor by asking someone well placed to keep you up to date on developments back home and to remind the right people in headquarters about you and what you're up to.

Staying on Headquarters' Radar Screen

Once overseas, try to keep a high profile, not because you crave attention but because you risk invisibility. At home you and your work get a certain amount of attention automatically, as a matter of course. To get the same amount of attention overseas, where there is virtually no mechanism for it to happen naturally, you will have to make a conscious effort. Write e-mails, faxes, quarterly activity reports, and semiannual and annual updates. Try to pass through headquarters whenever you can and drop in on people. Sign yourself up for task forces or committees that bring you in regular contact with people at headquarters. Prod your mentor to mention your name often. Persuade people from headquarters to pass through the field more often, even if only stopping by on the way to some other destination. Take at least part of your home leave back home; it may be less exciting than the Greek islands or the volcanoes of Costa Rica, but it's better for your career. Remember that in the end, there are only two kinds of visibility for an expatriate abroad: high and none.

If necessary, pester management about your reentry position. Remind them of the date of your return. Ask human resources what vacancies are opening up in the twelve months before your return and ask to be considered for appropriate ones. Although you can't immediately come back to take a new job, perhaps someone can fill in for you on an acting basis for two or three months.

Leave Right

Plan your departure from your overseas assignment. Wrap up loose ends, prepare your staff for the transition to the next regime, and make sure that any ongoing projects are in good hands. Nothing hurts a promising career more than to have a high-profile project you started suffer higher-profile collapse two months after you leave the country. Chances are very good that you, not your successor, will get the blame. Say good-bye to important people, planning ahead if necessary, so they're not out of town when it is time to bid them farewell. Set your replacement up for success, remembering that it is human nature to blame one's predecessor for every problem that occurs in the first six months.

Well before you depart, get your expectations about reentry out on the table where you can see them. What kind of job are you expecting? What kind of reception? How do you imagine friends and colleagues are going to view you? Are you assuming that you are basically the same person you were when you left? Are you expecting to have the same amount of authority, responsibility, and freedom in your new job that you had overseas? Are you expecting management to be as knowledgeable about and interested in the international side of the business as you are?

Back on the Job

Once you get home, be patient. Even the smoothest reentries have their rough spots. If you end up with a phantom job, use it as a base for getting the real job you would like to have. If you end up with a real job that doesn't suit you, give it some time. You may get used to it, you may be able to turn it into something that does suit you, or you can use it as a stepping-stone to something more suitable. Meanwhile, look for ways outside of your job but within the organization to use the skills and pursue the interests you acquired overseas. Volunteer for projects or task forces that need your international perspective and experience. Arrange to give presentations about the country or region you were in, about the overseas customers and markets, about what the foreign competition is doing. Help human resources find better ways to support expatriates and returnees. Become a mentor for the next generation of expats. Get involved in orienting foreign-bound employees and their families and in helping them come home. Start a newsletter for expats, the newsletter you would have liked to have received when you were abroad.

Think Back

Finally, as you go through reentry, remember that you have done this before (moved and changed jobs, that is) and lived to tell about it. You may even remember that you didn't adjust overnight that other time either. You should take comfort, then, in knowing that you probably have most of the skills it takes to weather this experience—the same skills you used last time—and that however difficult it may seem at the moment, in time you will begin to feel more relaxed and comfortable.

The Stages of Workplace Reentry

Just as returnees go through distinct stages of reentry in their personal lives (chapter 2), they go through the same process vis-à-vis their jobs and their employers. Workplace reentry consists of the same four stages and most of the same feelings and reactions presented in chapter 2 but with a different focus. In effect, then, we have already described the process and here need only relate key issues to the workplace setting. Returnees, of course, don't normally distinguish between the two environments or feel themselves going through two entirely separate reentries; rather, they see adjusting to work as just one more feature of the whole experience of coming home.

Leave-Taking

About six months before your departure, you will find yourself thinking in terms of bringing whatever issues or projects you're involved with to some kind of closure, and you may start to prepare someone else to take over in your absence, whether on an interim basis or as a permanent replacement. You will think about how you want to leave things when you go and begin arranging your affairs accordingly. At the same time you are not likely to initiate any new projects.

Your feelings at this stage will alternate between a strong desire to put this chapter of your life behind you and genuine regret at having to leave your colleagues and your job. You will probably wonder on occasion whether you are doing the right thing professionally by leaving, and you may begin to develop specific expectations about your new job.

The Honeymoon

If you are like most returnees, your first few weeks at work back at the home office are not especially demanding. Colleagues and friends are glad to see you, taking you out to lunch or dinner and asking what they can do to help. People take time to show you around, explain changes, introduce you to new people you need to know. Your secretary or support staff takes care of your logistical needs. People can't do enough for you.

Supervisors are also usually solicitous. They make a fuss over you, wine and dine you, and pick your brain. There may be a recognition event where your contribution abroad is celebrated and you are officially welcomed home. You may be asked to brief key people on what you learned overseas and be placed on committees or task forces dealing with international matters. In short you create quite a stir and feel rather special.

At the same time, very little is expected of you. People seem to understand that you are in transition, that you need time to settle in, both at home and at work. You may be given some leave without pay to get your personal affairs in order or be allowed to set your own hours. There is little pressure to perform—most things, it seems, can wait—and people are willing, if necessary, to make excuses for you.

At this stage you may have little sense of what your new job actually is, certainly not enough to know if you're going to like it or if it's going to put your recent international experience to use. For the most part you're really not doing your job yet, so you are not likely to have formed any opinions about it. Nor are you likely at this stage to miss the work you were doing abroad or the people you worked with or to make comparisons between abroad and home.

Reverse Culture Shock

In due time, you will stop circling your job and begin doing it. You will discover what your work actually consists of and what other people expect of you. Now you will see how much and what kind of authority and responsibility you have, over whom and over what, and whether your international experience is going to be used or valued. You will also begin having significant interactions with colleagues—interactions with real consequences, as opposed to the polite, superficial contact you have experienced up to now. You will see what your coworkers are like to work with, not just talk to, and you will also discover what they think of you. In other words this is the time when you begin to encounter many of the difficulties described in the rest of this chapter.

Because you have been away so long—or never worked in this particular division or location before—there will be much to learn. You will have few routines in the beginning, meaning everything is going to take more time and energy for you than it does for your colleagues, and you won't know many people well enough to have easy, relaxed interactions with them. Rather, most of your encounters will require considerable conscious attention and mental effort. You will be as tired by lunch as your coworkers are at day's end.

You are likely to be quite reactive and judgmental during this period, finding fault wherever you look. The way you learned to do things abroad will always seem better than how they are done here. You will chafe at how long it takes to get a decision out of people or to get something done once it has been decided. What you don't like about your organization and colleagues will stand out in bold relief, while anything you might like barely registers.

During this stage you will discover that you don't think or see things in quite the same light as most people at work do. A lot of your instincts—the ones you developed as an expatriate—may not serve you very well back in headquarters. You will be alone in many of your opinions and reactions, which will set you apart from your colleagues, and you may get a reputation for being "different." People who should listen to you do not. You will feel like the marginal person we described on page 54, and you may also be perceived as marginal by your colleagues.

Reverse culture shock at work is no more fun than it is away from work, and you may have many of the same reactions you are having in other areas of your life. You feel unappreciated, misunderstood, and forgotten. You may be frustrated or disillusioned; your self-confidence and self-esteem may plummet; and you may find yourself longing to be back overseas. You resist readjusting, equating it with suppressing or hiding the valuable knowledge and expertise you gained abroad. You think you have made a mistake in coming home, or at least in taking this particular job. You may think of leaving your company or organization and start looking for another employer. Nothing is working out quite the way you expected, and no one seems to understand how you feel or what you are going through.

Readjustment

While one-fourth of returnees change employers within a year of repatriation, many of the others eventually make peace with their new circumstances and arrive at the readjustment stage of reentry. At this point, you have reconciled yourself to the limitations or disappointments of your new position and may have discovered certain felicities that weren't apparent earlier. Your mood at work swings from being resigned to your job at one extreme to being pleased and excited at the other (just as it does for most people), but you don't think so much now about going back overseas or finding a new employer.

In a practical sense things are easier at work now. You have learned much of what you need to know to do your job well, and you have developed a number of routines that increase your efficiency. You know key people better—and they know you—so your interactions are smoother and easier. For these reasons you have more time and energy for your work and are able to make more significant contributions. Once you are out from under the minutiae of your new job, you may also see ways to put your international experience to use, either formally or informally.

Above all, you now have some perspective on your job, your organization, and your overseas experience, and you are accordingly able to see each of them more clearly. You can accept your boss and your colleagues for who they are and not keep wishing they were someone else. You realize that just as working back home has its rewards, so did working abroad have its limitations. And you realize that while it may have been difficult adjusting to your new job, that doesn't mean it was a mistake to have taken it.

4

The Return of
Spouses and Children

*Panama was my paradise. I really missed our live-in maid.
She was so good with the children. I didn't like having to
find baby-sitters back home or doing my own housework
again, for that matter.*

—Returning spouse

*I felt out of everything when I came back. I didn't know
about the music, what to wear, or how to get into the tight
cliques that have formed from people who have been together all their lives. My junior high school graduating class
in Saudi Arabia had just fifteen other kids. This high school
has 2,000 kids, and it is unbelievable.*

—Returning teenager

It has been estimated that 80 percent of all expatriates are married and 70 percent have children. If that is true, then a lot of
spouses and children are going through reentry. While spouses
and teenage children experience most of the adjustments described
in chapter 1, there are some additional issues that are unique to
these two groups. Younger children generally do not go through

the kind of reentry described earlier but nevertheless have their own set of adjustments. The special issues facing these three groups—spouses, teenagers, and younger children—are the subject of this chapter. For the most part the spouse we have in mind here is the nonworking partner of the expatriate employee, someone who did not work during the overseas sojourn and who is not returning to a job in his/her home country. Once again it is important to realize that there is no such thing as generic spouses or generic children, but there are a handful of adjustments that seem to apply to most returnees in these groups.

Issues for the Spouse

Work Matters

104

Some spouses return home to discover that they have to go—or go back—to work, that the family can not manage on the salary of one wage earner, especially if the family intends to live in the style to which it has become accustomed overseas. For spouses who have never worked, this is an enormous adjustment, a complete change of lifestyle. For spouses who worked before they went abroad and gave up a job or an entire career to accompany their partner to Los Angeles or Santiago, the necessity to go back to work is ironic at best and often a rude awakening besides. Many of these people have just gone through something of a struggle to adjust to not working, and now they have to turn around and gear up again for the workaday world. If they liked not working, then the adjustment will be considerable; if they didn't—many spouses are quite keen to restart their careers—then this aspect of reentry may be rewarding. Getting used to working is another book and not really our subject here, but suffice it to say that the number and variety of adjustments involved are considerable. When they are added to the other issues returnees face, the plot starts to thicken.

But we're getting ahead of ourselves. Adjusting to work is real enough, but first one has to find a job, which can be difficult for someone who has been out of the labor force for two or three years. In some fields a hiatus of this length is a serious obstacle to reemployment. In other cases age gets in the way, with the employer more inclined to hire a recent university graduate with similar skills and at half the cost. You may find you need special training before you will be truly competitive in your field again. Still another problem you may encounter is the reluctance of employers to hire someone who may very well have to quit in a year or eighteen months when that person's spouse gets posted abroad again.

If you reluctantly gave up a job and career to go overseas, being unable to find work upon reentry can be as much of an adjustment as having to work. While you may eventually have adjusted to not working overseas, upon coming home, you may be quite keen to press on with your career. If you are stymied in that effort, your self-esteem or identity may be threatened. You could justify not working overseas, maybe even come to enjoy it, but now that you have come home, you may feel pressure, from within and without, to resume your career. "The biggest challenge of coming home was going back to work again," one spouse from Finland observed. "Years without training and schooling resulted in a big career loss."

Home Alone

Families with children often come back in stages; the employee may have to come home early, the spouse staying behind until the children finish school, or the spouse may come ahead to enroll the children in school at the start of the school year. In the former instance, the spouse has to close down and pack up the overseas home on his or her own and see the children through this farewell stage alone. In the latter case, when spouse and children precede the employee, spouses have to go through reentry alone (both their own and that of the children) and make many important decisions without the advice of their partner. The sheer number of decisions that must be made can be overwhelming in itself, let alone the magnitude of them. You might have to decide which part of town to live in, choose a flat or a house, buy a car (and decide how much the family can now afford to spend on housing and a car), and find the school that is best for the children—decisions that have lasting consequences for the whole family. "I feel like the entire weight of our household is on my shoulders," one expat spouse observes. "Just strap the house, the moving van, the kids, and everything else on my back! I don't think it's very fair."

Shall I Bring the Tea Now, Memsahib?

Household servants are commonplace in many expatriate communities, but many families that can afford them overseas usually cannot back home. Indeed, the spectre of life without servants keeps many expats overseas longer than they had planned. And the reality makes many more want to get back overseas as soon as possible. Some expats even contrive to bring a much-loved servant with them when they return from abroad. Others, in contrast, are greatly relieved to put the servant "wars" behind them.

Whether you're relieved or shattered, the loss of servants means someone else is going to have to do whatever the servants were doing in Islamabad. While you ran your own household without giving it a thought before going overseas, you may not be taken with the prospect of doing so again. The fact is that most people adjust quite nicely to having other people do their housework and cooking. Even spouses who wonder with some urgency what they are going to do all day long in Cairo manage to adjust and somehow fill the day, so much so that they can't imagine where they will find the time and energy to run a household again. They may have come to enjoy, perhaps need, the pursuits and interests they cultivated abroad and now face having to give them up. They watch their freedom and independence evaporate before their eyes. A woman who lived in China writes,

> *In my own home it was expected, rightfully, that I would assume most of those housekeeping jobs that I had always done prior to [going to] China. But I did not want to settle down into my old life. I no longer wanted anything to do with domesticity because I realized in Daqing how much time had been freed for professional work when someone else took charge of the housekeeping. My household seemed unnecessarily complicated; managing it was a bore and an intrusion.*

Another consequence of the loss of servants is that the family may not entertain as often, with the result that at-home spouses now have less social contact with adults than they had abroad.

The Social Whirl

Expatriate communities tend to be closely knit and the social life highly organized, especially for spouses. There are all manner of committees and interest groups and a continuous string of special events. Spouses get used to coming together on a regular basis for recreational, educational, and service-oriented activities, which they find stimulating and satisfying. Back home, people seem to lead more independent lives and social interaction is not so structured. You may miss the frequent contact with other like-minded adults and the satisfaction of performing community service or the excitement of learning about Egyptian pottery. Such pursuits are usually possible back home, but they often require making more of a conscious effort. Meanwhile, if you have had to take over the household again, you may not have time for these activities, even if they are available.

Helping the Children

Another issue spouses have to contend with is the reentry of their children. While the employee is involved here as well, more of the responsibility inevitably falls to the spouse. As we will see in the rest of this chapter, reentry is not easy for children either, especially for teenagers, and it is the spouse who has to endure the lion's share of the acting out, bitterness, frustration, and drama that accompany a child's repatriation; likewise, the spouse must provide the lion's share of the comfort, support, reassurance, and understanding typically required at this juncture—all while struggling with his or her own reentry.

In some cases, children have an easy ride overseas, where the household help took over the chores that were the children's responsibility back home. While many parents guard against this development, with explicit instructions to servants, many others do not, with the result that when the family comes home, the children are out of the habit of helping around the house and not eager to resume their former chores.

Another matter spouses have to deal with upon reentry is the sudden reappearance of the employed spouse at the heart of the family. Many expatriate employees have to travel much more in their overseas assignment than in their position back home. They may also be required to work longer hours and entertain outside the home (when bigwigs visit). Typically, the at-home spouse fills the resulting void and takes on a much larger role in the rearing of the children and the running of the household. "I don't have any recollection of my father when we lived in Asia," one expat recalled. "He doesn't fit in. My mother was around a great deal, and I divided my time between her and the maid." Both you and the children get used to managing without the employed spouse—whose sudden return now disrupts all manner of well-established routines. You now have to make room for this new figure in your life and get used to sharing the decision making once again, and the children have to readjust to having two full-time parents.

Separate Ways

Many families find they spend much less time together upon reentry and are not as close. It is easier for teenagers in particular to lead more independent lives back home, where they have access to good public transportation (or even their own car) and can get around more easily on their own. Children have more options for their free time and don't spend as much of it at home, and the family in general does fewer things together. Parents who became used to their children being home every night for dinner and to knowing many of the details of their lives (the ones they're willing to reveal) now feel their children growing away from them. In the same way, spouses who were used to doing things for their children now find their children need them less. This happens in due course with all families, but it may happen more dramatically and suddenly with expatriate families upon reentry.

Fault Lines

Another issue that both parents have to face upon coming home is the guilt they feel for the hard time that preteens and especially teenagers have with reentry. While teens know it may not be the parents' "fault" that the family has to move back home, it *is* Mom's or Dad's job that has brought this misery upon them. The parents often have no more say in this matter than their children and are, in effect, as much victims as anyone else, but they are still likely to feel responsible for what has happened. "When my parents moved me back," one parent recalled of her own childhood,

> I was very angry. I'm sure they knew exactly how I felt, because I wasn't very subtle about it. Don't let this get to you. Your kids are just displacing their loneliness and anger and throwing it at you because you're the closest people to

*them. Remember that it's not anyone's fault, and it's espe-
cially not yours. It will pass and things will get better, but
give [children] lots of time.*

The Working Spouse May Not Understand

In some cases your return is complicated by the fact that your
spouse doesn't understand what you are going through. Not in the
sense that employed spouses aren't also going through reentry
(while contending with the return to work discussed in chapter
3), but in the sense that for all the adjustments the working spouses
must make, there is typically more structure to their day, and they
are doing a number of familiar things in a relatively familiar environment, perhaps with familiar people. In many cases the changes
in your routine and lifestyle, how you spend the day, are greater
and more numerous than those of the employee, who, as a consequence, may not always understand or be able to sympathize.
Moreover, the employed spouse may also not understand what you
are experiencing in trying to help the children readjust. "I don't
think my husband could relate to my problem," one returning
military spouse notes. "He had a job waiting for him at the Penta-
gon and a desk with his name on it." Another military wife noted
that "men have their built-in support group. They come back to a
familiar job, they wear the same uniform, and their basic day's
work is the same."

On the Other Hand

There are, of course, some things for you to look forward to about
being home. Many spouses feel like an appendage of the employee
when they're overseas, having gone abroad, after all, because that's
where their partners' careers took them. They don't have an identity in their own right so much as they are a part of someone else's
identity—and decidedly the lesser partner in the relationship. Ac-

cordingly, they may enjoy coming home and regaining their own identity.

Expat families often have to do a great deal of entertaining, inviting people into their homes whom they don't necessarily know, may not like, have nothing in common with, or would just rather not have to talk to on this particular evening. Since the spouses are usually at the center of such activity, it can be a relief not to be forced to give dinner parties all the time or to be charming to people they aren't fond of.

For some spouses, life in the expatriate community is too organized and inbred and too public. Everyone knows your business, your every move comes under close scrutiny, and there is no escape from the almost pathological socializing. Back home, you are freer to choose how much socializing you do, to decide how much you want to see of certain people, and mirabile dictu, to meet new people.

A related notion here is the fact that many expat spouses are obliged to live high-profile lives abroad, as official or unofficial representatives of the employee's country, company, or organization. In this role they have to be more than normally circumspect in their behavior and their conversation, for almost anything they do or say may reflect, for better or worse, on the country or the employer. Many spouses enjoy the return to anonymity, where they can let down their guard and speak their mind with relative impunity.

What Spouses Can Do

You should try to plan for repatriation well before it happens, beginning with deciding whether you will need or want to work when you return. If you will, you should be preparing for that day from the time you arrive overseas, keeping up with developments in your field by subscribing to professional journals, attending conferences and workshops, taking classes by mail, and getting any other training that will keep you professionally competitive. Home leave is an especially useful time to take courses and seminars, buy the latest books, and talk to people in your field.

Home leave is also the time to lay more serious groundwork for your return by setting up interviews with potential employers and reactivating your professional networks. You should also find out what your spouse's company offers in the way of support. If it offers nothing, maybe your higher-ups will be agreeable to starting something now. The human resources team in your spouse's organization certainly knows human resources people in other organizations and may be able to help you through their network. Staying in touch from overseas is hard; enlisting someone in your cause back home can be very helpful.

Spouses who have to cope with the loss of household help don't have many choices. They can entertain less, enlist the help of the employed spouse and older children, and perhaps hire a cleaning person who comes in once a week or so. Spouses who miss the many outside activities they were involved in overseas can join organizations and interest groups in their community or take adult education courses. Families who miss the closeness they enjoyed abroad can establish one or two evenings a week when they will plan to eat dinner together.

The reappearance of the absentee parent in the life of the household normally calls for some negotiating. Husband, wife, and older children should decide what role each is going to play in the newly reconstituted family. In particular, everyone needs to be clear about who gets what duties. If the wife, for example, has taken over as the disciplinarian in the husband's absence, these two need to decide who gets this job now, and then let the children know. The same goes for other family responsibilities, such as decisions about money, liaison with the children's school, helping with homework, and all the common household duties.

You should try to find other spouses who have been through reentry. There are likely to be some at your overseas post who can tell you what the experience is like and give you some good advice. Still more important, try to find returned spouses back home. There may be other returnee families in your spouse's organization, but if there aren't, look in the wider community. You don't have to know these people in order to call on them; people who have been through reentry have an instant rapport with each other, whether they've ever met or not.

As we have been saying throughout this book, get your expectations and assumptions about reentry out on the table where you can examine them. Just what do you see yourself doing upon your return? What is the job market like in your field? What will your role be vis-à-vis your children? What does the family financial picture look like? If you have had household help overseas, what's going to happen now that you are going home? How is your lifestyle going to change? How much free time are you going to have? What will your spouse be going through? What expectations does your family back home have of you?

Issues for Younger Children

The reentry experience for children varies with their age; in general, the more the child has a life outside the home, the more complicated reentry becomes. For very young children, from birth to five years, reentry is just like any other move—and very much like the move abroad. School-age children, from six to twelve, will have a number of school-related adjustments. And teenagers (see next section) are in a class all their own.

Nothing Is Familiar

Young children are comforted by the familiar and the routine, which is not exactly what reentry is all about. At a minimum relocating means a new room, a new house or flat, a new neighborhood, a new school or preschool, and all manner of new people. In many cases it means temporary separation from one parent, usually the employee, either because the family does not return together or because the working parent has to travel extensively upon reentry. In some cases, as we have seen, reentry means the spouse has to go to work, which means that both parents are absent much of the time. In short, reentry has the potential of turning a child's world upside down, depriving him or her of the familiar people, places, and things that are the main source of a child's sense of security and well-being.

For some small children reentry is complicated by the sudden separation from a beloved nanny or servant. While we tend to think of the parents, especially the mother or at-home spouse, as the key adults in a child's world—and their presence, therefore, as a great source of comfort and security upon reentry—expat children raised by a nanny may in fact be leaving behind the key adult in their life.

Symptoms

The signs of a difficult reentry are the usual signs of insecurity among small children: clinging to the parents, including hysterical behavior when the parents go out for the evening or one parent leaves on a business trip; the usual attention-getting behaviors, including fussiness, crying, and eating problems; regressive behavior such as thumb sucking, asking for a bottle, bed-wetting; and other signs of stress, such as irritability, sleeping problems, toilet-training difficulties, and refusal to take naps.

What Parents Can Do for Younger Children

Easing reentry for young children is a matter of making them feel secure and safe again, and that means trying to restore as much familiarity and routine to their world as possible. A child's room is a good place to start—and the sooner you start, the better. You may live in a different flat or house (or in the same place, but your child might not remember it), with all manner of strange rooms, corridors, sounds, smells, and surfaces. The child's room may not be similar to the one he or she has just left, but you can fill it with the child's favorite animals, toys, games, drawings, videos, picture books, and furniture to give the child a sense of continuity and stability. In this regard, be careful when packing up to leave the overseas post not to throw away any of the sacred objects your child clings to when he or she is upset.

If possible, before the family moves, show the children pictures or videotapes of their new home—their new room, the yard (if there is one), and the street. This will make their new surroundings seem more familiar when the family arrives, especially since children typically ask to look at these pictures or videos over and over. The same can be done for the school or preschool the child will be attending. Obtain pictures of the rooms, building, and the teachers.

The presence of familiar people other than the parents, of course, can also be a great comfort to small children: grandparents, other relatives, and friends (provided the children are old enough to remember them). If not, then these strangers who suddenly appear out of nowhere and want to hug them and hold them on their laps will be just one more frightening change to deal with. Here again, pictures will help to prepare children for the grandparents they may have forgotten, as will stories (with photos if possible) reminding your children of events they shared with their relatives.

In the end the parents, a child's single greatest source of security, are the key to a successful relocation. Your physical presence on a regular, predictable basis will do more than any other single factor to calm children's fears about this strange new world and reassure them that they will be safe here. For this reason, both parents should be home as much as possible during the first two or three months of reentry. The working spouse, in particular, should try to minimize business travel during this period.

Not only should the parents be present, they should also try not to show any outward signs of the stress, anxiety, or frustration they may be feeling about being home and going through reentry. Children will sense when a parent is unhappy and this will only increase their anxiety and fear. As Joel Wallach and Gale Metcalf have noted, "Smaller children, who may not ordinarily be affected by the reentry process, [sometimes] pick up the stress their parents are experiencing and exhibit it in any number of ways, ranging from bad conduct at home or school to regressive, withdrawn behaviors."

116

Issues for Teenagers

Research shows that teenagers have the most difficult reentry of any age group. Teenage years aren't easy under the best of circumstances, but when you throw reentry into the volatile mix of physical, psychological, and emotional changes teenagers are going through, it's no wonder the pot boils over.

Not Fitting In

The most serious reentry issue for teenagers is not fitting in with their peers back home. In one survey 93 percent of returning teenagers said they did not feel at home among their peers. When you consider that being accepted by their peers is perhaps the greatest need of teenagers, then not fitting in becomes a serious matter. Moreover, psychologists agree that in the teenage years self-acceptance, an essential cornerstone for normal psychological and emotional development, is in large part a function of being accepted by others.

In teen years, being accepted means being like one's peers, that is, conforming to the norms of the group and not standing out. The three basic prerequisites here are dressing the way other teens dress, talking about what everyone else talks about, and talking the way other teens do. For the returnee, who has been away two or three years, this may not be easy.

Dress Matters

For teenagers clothes are highly significant, not so much in their own right but for what wearing the right clothes says about the person. It suggests that you understand that people will be judged by what they wear and, more importantly, that you care about that judgment. As long as you care about what others think, as long as you demonstrate that you are willing and able to conform, then you can be trusted. And once you can be trusted, then you can be accepted. Clothes were no doubt important in your teenager's overseas school too, but chances are, what was "in" in Oslo or Seoul may not be "in" back in London or Boston. "Just recently I got back from Greece," a teen observes, "where it was the in thing to wear leather sandals. When I came back, everyone had their big-name sneakers, and I had my worn-out sandals. I was questioned a lot about why I wore strange shoes, and I soon gave them up for Nikes." The right clothes don't guarantee acceptance, of course, but without them your son or daughter isn't even in the running.

117

Behind on Popular Culture

With some advance planning and a lot of cash, teens can usually manage to look like other teens, but talking about what other teens talk about may be harder to pull off. Overseas, they may not have been able to keep up on the latest singers and music groups, sports figures, film and TV personalities and shows, video games,

Websites, brand names, fast foods, and "in" places. These matters are the preoccupation and obsession of most teens, and not to know about them is almost like not being a teen. At best, the returnee's ignorance dooms him or her to being a listener and not a participant in most conversations; at worst, it excludes the teen from being accepted by other teens or at least delays acceptance for some time.

Teen Talk

Talking "teen" is the third sine qua non of being accepted. Other teens might overlook the fact that the returning teen has never seen a certain music video or watched a certain TV show or visited a particular Website—after all, that can be their little secret—but they are unforgiving if the returnee doesn't know how to talk "teen." Quite simply, if one doesn't speak or understand their language, one can't really fit in. Moreover, returnees stand to embarrass them with their friends if they find out this new teen doesn't know how to talk right. While returning teens pick up teen talk as fast as they can, they don't always arrive speaking it, and among teenage peer groups, first impressions can be fatal.

A Sheltered Life

Because of the sheltered life in some expat communities, there may be common aspects of teenage life that returnees know nothing about, which also makes them stand out from their peers. As expatriates, they may never have had summer or part-time jobs and earned their own money. They may never have baby-sat or learned how to drive (which is especially important in the United States). They may know how to change planes at Heathrow or how to bargain with merchants in Cairo, but they may never have used an ATM machine, don't have a cell phone, and have never bought a condom.

Cliques

Returning teens are also at a disadvantage because by and large teen life in expatriate communities was not very cliquish. This is partly because international schools tend to be much smaller and also because in overseas schools, everyone is an outsider, or at least a very recent outsider, and teens therefore tend to be more inclusive and accepting of someone who is new or different. In this atmosphere, there is less breaking up into groups, and most teens interact regularly with most other teens (of their same grade, at least), not just with a select few. Returnees, then, are not used to being kept at a distance because they are different or to having to cultivate relationships in order to be accepted.

Many returning teens are approached and befriended by teens who are outsiders themselves, who have never been accepted by the more mainstream, desirable groups. Sometimes these are teens with drug, alcohol, or other behavioral problems who seek out other fringe people like themselves whom they can bond with and influence. Returnees are especially vulnerable in this regard, for they have no group they obviously belong to. To be identified with these people often makes it difficult for returnees to be accepted by those whose approval they seek. "Everybody sat there and looked at me," one teen remembers,

119

> *and at what I was wearing. You get to the point where you'll be friends with anybody who's friendly to you. One of the guys who was friendly to me wasn't the kind of person I really like. He was into drugs and bad-mouthed everything about the school. But I was lucky because later I got to be friends with some other people.*

Threatened Peers

In some cases returnees aren't accepted because their peers are threatened by them. The returnee speaks another language, has been to Paris and Hong Kong, has skied in the Alps, and has spent the summer on a Greek island. The self-confidence of many teens is a gossamer kind of skin, easily undermined by someone who has done and seen much more than the teen back home may ever do or see. Teens who are put on the defensive won't hesitate to strike out. "What you gained from [the] experience abroad is going to be maintained," one teen notes, "but it's better to tuck it away. What you learned not only doesn't get you anywhere, it tends to threaten or irritate people."

Do I Really Want to Fit In?

The whole problem of fitting in is complicated by another dilemma: there may be things about their peers back home that returning teens find profoundly troubling, making the prospect of fitting in something of a dubious distinction. For one thing teens back home often seem insular and narrow-minded. They can be appallingly ignorant of any country other than their own and quick to judge other cultures as inferior. "I was wearing an 'I love Tokyo' pin," one teen recalled, "and someone made a remark about it and asked if I spoke Chinese. They didn't even know that Japanese is a separate language. No one was at all enlightened [about] foreign countries or the world in general."

Returning American teens in particular are often appalled at the materialism of their peers back home, especially returnees whose parents were posted in developing countries. Returning teens may also be taken aback by certain cultural traits that they have either lost or forgotten about overseas: people may be too direct or not direct enough, they may be too competitive or not competitive enough, they may talk too loud or too soft, or they may stand too close (or too far) and touch too much (or too little).

Expat teens are often quite mature and sophisticated for their age, having traveled extensively, learned another language, and generally spent more time than their at-home counterparts in the company of adults. They may relate better to adults than to people their own age, especially their so-called peers back home, who often strike returnees as immature and shallow. "I felt I was more mature than the other kids," one returnee wrote, "and the things they thought were important seemed trivial to me. What am I going to wear to school today? Who am I going to walk home with? Those are just not big things in my life." Returning teens often feel more comfortable with teens who are two or three years older than they, but it is not always easy to be accepted by these people. Older teens normally don't find it amusing to be chatted up by younger ones.

Some returnees are put off, even scared, by the amount of drug and alcohol use among their peers and by their casual attitude toward sex. While expat teens are often more mature and sophisticated than peers back home, they have also been more protected in some respects.

Fitting in also poses another, related kind of identity problem: being accepted means they have to give up or at least hide some of the values and attitudes they acquired overseas, the qualities that now set them apart. In other words, fitting in means having to deny at least part of who teens think they are. If they should happen to like those parts of themselves, then hiding or denying them in order to fit into a society they're having some doubts about anyway may not be particularly appealing or healthy.

So it is that teenage returnees' feelings about fitting in are genuinely conflicted. On the one hand, they want—and need—to be liked and accepted by their peers; on the other hand, they are appalled at some of the values and behaviors of these very same people. In some ways, not fitting in with such people is practically a badge of honor.

Friends Have Changed

Teens don't return completely friendless, of course. Most still have the friends they left behind when they went abroad, some of whom they may have seen regularly during home leave. But acceptance by one's friends isn't automatic. For one thing, some best friends may now have new best friends made in one's absence, just as the teen probably made a new best friend overseas. Moreover, both returnees and their friends have changed and may no longer have much in common or enjoy each other's company. Returnees may be disappointed to find that their friends now seem boring. On the other hand, friends back home may think the returnee has become conceited since he or she went abroad. Even if none of this is true, distance and the passage of time inevitably strain even the strongest relationships, as one teen has recalled.

> *When I left [home], I had one best friend and many other close friends. When I came back, they were still my good friends, but now they were all best friends because they went through so much together last year when I was away. I still feel left out sometimes, and it's going to take time before I fit in again.*

"I still feel like kind of an outsider," another teen recalls, "when they say 'Remember when...,' and I never remember because I wasn't there!"

School

Because school is the center of teen life, it's not surprising that adjusting to a new school is another major problem of reentry. Just being new is difficult, as we have observed earlier, as is the sudden loss of identity, of going from being the best student in math, the clown of physics class, or the editor of this or the president of that to being a virtual nonentity. Since the typical expat school is a private international school and is usually much smaller than the schools back in one's home country, returning teens have to adjust to being one of seven hundred or a thousand students instead of one out of seventy-five or a hundred. The feeling of being anonymous, virtually invisible, is hard for teens who most likely had a high profile in their expat school.

On the whole, teens who attend expat schools are used to not only much smaller classes, more individual attention, and generally a much closer relationship with their teachers but also a higher quality of education. The teachers are better, the students are more motivated and disciplined, there is more homework, and the academic standards are higher. Private schools back home offer this kind of education, of course, but returning families typically cannot afford to send their children to such schools, which were, after all, paid for by the employer or by the government when the family was overseas. In some cases returnees are able to skip grade levels, which may be good for their educational advancement but not necessarily for their social adjustment. Another frustration for some teens is finding themselves, by virtue of the richness of their overseas experience, to be in many ways more knowledgeable and sophisticated than their teachers back home.

123

Larger schools also mean more competition for academic and athletic distinction. A boy who could play forward on the expat soccer team might not make the second team back home. A girl whose singing was good enough to get her the lead in *Grease* overseas might not make it into the chorus in her new school back home. "I wasn't a super jock," one returnee remembers, "which was a prerequisite for any sport [back home]. At my international school, if you knew what a basketball looked like, you could play on the team."

How Interesting

Teens also find it disappointing that no one is interested in their overseas experiences. Peers, as well as adults, ask few questions, don't listen very long when you start talking, and don't necessarily understand when they do listen. Even friends don't seem that interested. As these have often been formative experiences, not being able to share them with others leaves teens feeling that their friends no longer know them. "When I try to tell people what it was like," one teen observes, "it probably sounds like I just want them to envy me. But it's not that. I just want them to know what I felt [and] who I am."

Missing Life Abroad

Teens also miss much about their life abroad, starting with their friends. Many teens leave a girlfriend or boyfriend behind. Expat friends tend to spend more time in the exclusive company of each other than do home-culture friends because there are fewer places to go and mix with other teens. As a result, friendships may be more intense. Teens and younger children may also miss a much-loved servant, teacher, or family friend. Many teens find great pleasure in learning and speaking a new language and feel almost as if a part of their identity has been taken from them when they can no longer use it. As anyone who has learned another language can attest, the experience is like taking on another self; one has a certain persona in one's mother tongue and another, often very different, persona in the foreign language. Take away that foreign language—and that other person disappears right along with it. "I'm two people," a returning teen observes. "The one who uses English is quiet and precise; the Portuguese one gestures and is poetic and free."

Teens may also miss the notoriety they had overseas, the sense of standing out and feeling unique. Suddenly, there's no special response when they stroll down the sidewalk or into a shop. "Over there you walk down the street," one teen recalled, "and everyone looks at you. You're on stage all the time. Back [home] you miss all the attention. You become an unperson."

Disappearing Parents

Another adjustment teens and preteens must make is to the general lack of adult supervision back home. In expat communities, working couples are usually the exception, which means there is usually an adult around when children bring their friends home. Parents overseas are also more likely to drive kids to social and recreational events and to pick them up afterward. Back home, teens can often get around much more easily on their own, and parents may not be at home until after work. While many teens no doubt welcome this freedom and independence, it may be more than some of them can handle.

Dependent Again

Another complication of reentry is that it tends to make teens at least temporarily more dependent on their parents than they would like to be. They may need to have Mom or Dad drive them places, at least at first. They may not fit in with peers yet or have had time to make friends, with the result that they will depend more on their parents for approval and emotional support. Yet teens know this isn't quite right; the teenage years are the time when they should be more involved with their friends than their parents. "During reentry," Rita Siebenaler has written of American teens,

> *the young adult becomes more dependent on parents, when the opposite would be more developmentally appropriate. The whole adolescent struggle for independence is at odds with the needs of re-entering teenagers. Healthy development requires a degree of independence which is much more difficult to achieve when the adolescent is forced to rely on the family as the sole source of continuity and support amidst change.* (1988, 53)

Figure 4.1
Symptoms of Reentry Shock in
Older Children and Teenagers

It's never easy to know the real reason children behave the way they do, but there are some common signs of reentry shock. If your older child or teenager exhibits these behaviors, it may be at least in part because of the trials of coming home.

1. Regressive behavior: almost anything the child/teen used to do but has since grown out of.
2. Recurring minor maladies: the emotional stress of reentry makes some children/teens more prone to getting sick.
3. Proneness to accidents: this may be regressive behavior, a simple lack of self-confidence, or the manifestation of a need for extra attention.
4. Withdrawal: wanting to be alone.
5. Sudden drop in school marks: the child/teen is too troubled to concentrate or has low self-esteem, which affects performance.
6. Irritability: the child/teen angers easily, has no patience.
7. Change in leisure activities.
8. Change in eating habits.
9. Change in sleeping habits.

126

It Won't Get Better

It is important to remember that preteens and teenagers (and young children more so) are not as prone as adults to take the long view of things or even to realize there is one. They live in the here and now, thinking that what is now is pretty much what will be. They don't have enough experience to understand and take comfort from the fact that things are going to change, to get better. Hence, they experience present circumstances and reality with an intensity that those who can distance themselves are spared. In other words, everything looks worse to them than it does to their parents, who may thus underestimate their child's feelings and not be as supportive as they need to be.

Figure 4.2
The Value of the Overseas Experience

When children, especially teenagers, are suffering through reentry, complaining that this would never have happened if they had just stayed home (all of which, by the way, is your fault, parents), remind them of what they gained, of how much they have benefited from living overseas.

1. They may have learned a new language, which will be useful in later life.
2. They visited many wonderful places that they would otherwise never have seen.
3. They made new friends and had exciting experiences.
4. They have an understanding of and tolerance for differences.
5. They have had a very good education (the university entrance exam scores of expat children are well above average) and have a better chance of being admitted to a good university.
6. They are savvy about traveling.
7. They are more confident with adults and more sophisticated.
8. They are more flexible and learn quickly.
9. Their international experience will one day make them more attractive to employers.

What Parents Can Do for Teenagers

Predeparture

Ideally, helping teenagers through reentry begins overseas, long before the family comes home. A place to start is to make sure teens get the latest popular-culture magazines from home, with information on all the latest fashions, musicians and groups, TV shows, films, and personalities. Copies of the latest music videos and tapes of the hot TV shows are also good reentry study material. This will allow teens to understand and be able to talk about what other teens are talking about and to learn some of the "in" phrases and slang.

Visits home probably do more than any other single thing to prepare teens for reentry. Visits turn into a kind of reconnaissance of the home culture, letting teens get the lay of the land in advance of the real return. Time at home also exposes teens and preteens to some of the reactions and attitudes they will face later and some of the feelings they will have. In addition these visits allow teens to catch up with their friends back home, and vice versa, thus making the eventual reentry less jarring. If circumstances permit and such visits are planned properly, they can do still more. Teens can take a job during an extended stay, the summer vacation, for example. Ideally, this visit will take place in the town the teen will be returning to. There is one caveat here, however, which is to remind teens that while visiting back home may give them a useful preview of the culture and some of the experiences that await them upon reentry, it is profoundly different from living there.

Sometimes, with advance planning, parents can arrange to send their children to a school of the same size as the one they attended overseas. If the family is returning to a new community, parents should inquire about the available schools and, where practical, plan to live in a neighborhood with a smaller school. For families where it is an option, a private school can make for a softer landing. Some thought has to be given to this decision, however, if the child was not in a private school before going abroad. The benefits of the private school must be weighed against the advantages of putting the children back in the school they already know and where their friends are enrolled.

Older children should be told about reverse culture shock before it happens to them. Parents can talk with their children about the issues presented here, and teens and preteens can be invited to participate in reentry workshops held overseas by the employer. In many expat communities, there may be teens with peers who have already gone through reentry and who could lead a discussion on the experience. Teenagers who have just arrived from the home country can help by filling in departing teens on the latest in teen culture.

Before the family leaves to come home, parents should make sure their preteen and teenage children have a chance to say goodbye to friends and other important people. Parents can arrange sleep-overs and farewell parties. If a child has fought with a best friend or otherwise feels bad about a particular relationship, parents should encourage the child to patch things up before leaving.

129

After the Return

When the family is back home, there are other things that can be done. Once again, it helps for parents themselves to be positive about reentry, at least on the outside, and also to be aware of some of the common signs of culture shock in children (see Figure 4.1, page 126). One necessity for returning teens is to be allowed to make long, and usually very expensive, telephone calls to their friends overseas. Until they make new friends back home, teens and preteens need that contact with old friends that reassures them they are indeed liked and accepted by people their own age—that at least they belong overseas even if they don't yet seem to belong back home. They can send e-mail, too, of course, as well as chat on electronic networks. Parents should likewise not skimp on buying clothes for their children, especially teenagers.

Wherever possible, you should try to put your teens in touch with others who have gone through reentry. Such children are an instant peer group, even if they are complete strangers. What matters is that they understand what your child is going through and can offer reassurance that he or she is not the first or last person to go through this. If your company or organization regularly posts people abroad, then there is already a group of such teens to contact. Parents will normally have to take the lead in this, for teens aren't likely to call up complete strangers and ask them to dinner; indeed, they may beg their parents not to do this to them. There may also be in your area a chapter of Global Nomads, International, an organization for young people who have lived for some years outside their passport country because of a parent's employment abroad (see page 190 for address).

You can also try to help your children take the long view of things. Remind them how they felt when they first arrived in the overseas city, how they thought then that they would never be happy there, and how much they wanted to go home. At the same time parents can remind their children of the many benefits of living overseas. Sure, it set them up for the misery they feel now and hardly seems worth the pain, but it was still a very valuable experience they shouldn't regret and the value of which will one day be apparent to them (see Figure 4.2, page 127).

Teens who miss speaking the foreign language they have learned and having contact with people from other cultures can join or start an international club or encourage their families to host an exchange student. They can also sign up for a language class at the local community center or language school.

If parents can afford it, granting unhappy returnees their fondest wish and sending them back to visit their friends overseas after six to nine months of being away generally closes the book on a lot of reentry issues. Teens discover that time has not stopped in their absence: some friends may have moved away; others now have new best friends; and all of them have changed. They can visit a beloved servant, who is touched and happy to see them, but now he or she is serving new people and doesn't have much time for reliving fond memories. Teachers too are happy to see their old students (if the teacher hasn't moved on), but one can't help noticing that there is a new Michael or Sylvia who has taken one's place as the best geography student or the new hope of the tennis team. Such a visit back in time is not all rude awakenings, but there are enough that parents should caution children about them before sending them off.

One thing you might want to avoid telling older children, especially teenagers, is that you know what they are going through—because you don't, unless you grew up in an expatriate family. You were a teenager once, of course, and may remember those years with startling clarity, but you have probably never been through many of the adjustments your child now faces. This doesn't mean you can't be sympathetic and supportive, but it does mean you can't completely understand the feelings your child may be having or always be able to offer useful advice. As Sidney Werkman has observed,

> The youngster growing up overseas often must move during adolescence...[and] as a result must make many individual, often lonely decisions that define his being. He cannot fall back upon parental experience for guidance, as his parents have grown up in a different societal situation, typically that of the [home culture]." (1979, 178–89)

One returning teen wrote the following in a letter to her parents:

A particular aspect of my "heritage" is that unlike most, it's not a shared one. I don't have anyone to swap notes with, if you know what I mean. Even you and Daddy experience things in a radically different way—you were adults and already formed, while I was a child, malleable, susceptible, and unmolded. [This] uniqueness, while precious, is also very lonely at times.

Nor do parents experience the rejection or ridicule that their children sometimes go through upon reentry. Other adults may not understand what reentry is and what you're struggling with, but they aren't unkind about it. Adults "have mature adults around to talk to," one returning parent has written.

Kids are not as mature or accepting, and they may be rejecting your child at school. Your kids may go through social hell, and there's nothing anyone can do about it. Be understanding, but realize that that doesn't mean you know what it's like.

You will do your very best, of course, to help your children through this experience—and your very best will quite often be good enough—but at times you will have to let them find their own way through the trials of reentry.

What Teens Can Do

While your parents can help make your reentry a lot easier, there are also a number of things you can do to help yourself. When you are still overseas, keep in touch with teen life and popular culture back home. Be sure to read magazines that will keep you up to date on the latest TV shows, films, music groups, fashion trends, and all the other things you will be expected to know about when you return. Ask your friends to keep you posted on the latest fads, slang, and popular hangouts—not because these fads, expressions, and hangouts will necessarily still be important when you get back, but because you will at least know what your friends are talking about when they refer to these things in conversation.

Stay in touch with your friends back home. Call them (if your parents allow you) and e-mail them often, so they aren't strangers to you—and you to them—when you go back. You will still have to renew those friendships once you come home, but at least you won't have to start from scratch. Moreover, if you tell friends back home about your experiences while you are still abroad, you may not have such a strong urge to monopolize conversation when you return.

In countries where it's important, be sure to learn how to drive. If you will be old enough to drive when you get home, your friends will expect you to be able to do so. If you can't drive legally in the country where you're living, you may be able to take lessons and practice.

You may want to be low-key about your overseas experiences when you first get back. Your friends may be threatened or think you are bragging when you talk about all the places you went and the things you did when you lived in Sao Paulo or Singapore. "Get some friends," one returning teen advised, "get your foothold in the school and don't tell everyone about your life experiences. Don't lie about them, but don't talk about them too much. They may not understand. In my case the students had no way to relate to me because I was coming from such a different world." Meanwhile, be sure to ask your friends about what has happened in their lives while you were gone.

Don't judge other teens too harshly. They might seem superficial or prejudiced, shockingly ignorant about other countries and cultures, or just not interested in the world outside your home country. They may make fun of you because of your overseas experience or because you don't know what clothes to wear or who a popular singer is. If you can grin and bear all this, it may pass. These teens may be threatened by you and are just trying to cut you down to size. Once they've stopped acting defensive, they

133

might turn out to be nice people. "The hardest thing for me," one returning American teen observed,

> has been to keep from criticizing American kids. So many seem interested only in drinking and "getting laid." I just cannot relate to this. I often criticize American materialism and wastefulness. But there are many good characteristics which Americans hold dear, and I try hard to dwell on the good rather than the bad. I know if I criticize them, then I am just as guilty as they are when they criticize other cultures and values.

Don't be too hard on your parents either. It's not really their fault that you're having to go through reentry; it's just a situation that can't be avoided, by them or by you. Meanwhile, remember that reentry may not be much fun for them either. As one returning teen has noted,

> Chances are your parents are having a hard time...as well. Often kids do not take this into consideration, thinking that their parents moved away from their old home just to hurt them. This is not true at all, and it takes awhile for kids to realize this. Whatever the reasons for the move, you should not take your emotions out on your mom or your dad.

While you are going through reentry, you will want to stay in touch with your friends from overseas. If they are still abroad, perhaps you can call them (this may depend on the family budget) or talk via e-mail. If they are from your home culture and have returned, you may be able to visit them.

You should also seek out other teens in your town or school who are returnees like yourself. You may not know these teens, but you will still have a lot in common. Ask your parents if there are people at work who lived overseas and whose children you could arrange to meet.

Remember that it takes time to fit back in and be accepted, to feel as if you belong back in your home country. While it's perfectly normal to feel lonely and depressed in the beginning and to want to go back overseas, this is going to change. This is emphatically not how you will feel in a few weeks or how you are always going to view your country and your peers. Nor is this always how other teens are going to treat you and react to you. In other words, adjusting back home doesn't mean that you just have to get used to feeling lonely and homesick or simply learn to live with being an outsider. This is a phase, and it will pass (see chapter 2 on the stages of reentry). "When would I ever get a grip on the situation that was ruining my life?" one returning teen asked herself.

> *The answer to that question came when I tried out for the spring musical and got a part. I suddenly was no longer an outsider. I had an identity and I had a name people knew. Those awful months of feeling so alone and so weird were over, just like that.*

135

Not only will you adjust in due time, but once you do, you will begin to cherish the overseas experience, the very same overseas experience that is the reason for so much suffering during the early stages of reentry. "The experience was something my grandfather would say was character building," the teenager quoted above notes.

> *Growing up internationally...is a way of life that never leaves you, no matter where you live. It is in your blood and it becomes a part of you, and you pass it on to your kids if they are lucky. It has been hard and it has been fun, and I wouldn't trade my life for anything.*

Another returnee, speaking of her life abroad, put it more simply: "I have sauntered away with riches."

5

Special Populations

Thus far in these pages we have painted reentry with rather a broad brush, identifying issues common to most returnees regard- less of how they spent their time as expatriates or of the situations they are returning to. Even the distinctions we have made up to now, in chapters 3 and 4, have deliberately been as broad as possible. Chapter 3 looks at common issues facing *anyone* who returns to his or her previous place of work, and chapter 4 describes the return of the "typical" spouse and "typical" children. We know, of course, that typical people don't actually exist, but we trust that readers will nevertheless recognize themselves now and again in these pages.

In this chapter, we depart from our generic approach and explore issues relevant to special populations. In each case what makes the particular group special is the unique nature of their overseas experience—the circumstances under which they live and work—which in turn makes certain aspects of their reentry also unique. This is not to say that people in these groups do not have most of the experiences described elsewhere in these pages, but only that they may also have other reentry experiences that either we have not addressed or that we have discussed but which manifest for this group in an unusual way or with an unusual intensity.

We should remember that even here, with these so-called special populations, there is still tremendous diversity. No two exchange students leave from or return to the same set of circumstances or have the same experience overseas. Some international volunteers serve in Budapest and others serve in the Kalahari Desert. Some military personnel return to rural Georgia and others to London. There are no generic experiences to be had here anymore than there are in the rest of this book, and we beg the reader's indulgence accordingly.

I. Exchange Students

It was really hard. I was happy to see my family and friends here [in Ecuador], but part of my heart is still in Upper Peninsula [Michigan].
—Ecuadorian exchange student

Each year tens of thousands of high school students spend part or all of an academic year in a foreign country or several weeks in a summer abroad program. From the United States alone, between twenty and forty thousand teenagers go abroad on such programs annually, and twice that number of foreign students come to the United States on exchanges. The numbers are similar, and in some cases higher, for exchanges between other countries. And sooner or later, of course, these students come home and go through reentry.

In some respects returning exchange students are like anyone who comes home from abroad (see chapter 1); in other respects they are like returnees of their particular age group (see the section on teenagers in chapter 4); and in still other ways their experience is unique to their status as reentering exchange students. It is this latter set of issues we will examine in this section.

We should begin by distinguishing returning exchange students from other returnees, and especially from other returning students (the teenagers discussed in chapter 4). With few exceptions, exchange students go overseas by themselves; they do not go with their families (like most expat teenagers) or in groups or even to communities where there are other students like themselves. Unlike expat students, these students do not attend private international schools, where everyone is just like them, but enroll in the national schools of the host country—where few or none are quite like them. Moreover, unlike most expat students who have little say about going abroad, exchange students make a conscious choice to go overseas.

For all of these reasons, the overseas experience of the exchange student is significantly different from that of students who merely accompany their family abroad and end up going to school overseas. It's no wonder, then, that the return and reentry experience of these two kinds of students would also be very different.

The most salient difference, no doubt, is that while expat students return *with* their family, exchange students return *to* their family. And therein lies a tale.

The Issues

The Parent Problem

Learning to live again with one's family, and especially with one's parents, is probably the most significant aspect of exchange student reentry—and one of the most charged. On the one hand students are excited to see their parents again and bursting with stories to tell, and parents are happy and excited to have their children back home. At the same time the two parties have not inhabited the same universe for several months (or a year) and are not used to each other's company. They can and will get into the habit of being together again, but the transition can be rocky.

139

Probably the greatest frustration for returning exchange students is the sudden reappearance of their parents in their lives, not the actual individuals but in their roles as father and mother. The issue here is not that these students feel they no longer need their parents, but that they may feel they don't need them quite as much as they did before they left. Compared with their peers who stay at home, most exchange students mature at an accelerated pace during the course of their overseas sojourn. Because of the numerous challenges exchangees face and overcome as they adjust to living thousands of miles from home in a new country and to functioning in a new language, they are likely to be more independent and self-assured than others their age and more so than their parents were at the same age—and significantly, more so than their parents expect them to be when they return. Moreover, in many cases the host father and mother may not have become as involved in as many aspects of the exchange student's life as natural parents are inclined to be and may not have been as strict.

Your parents, of course, can't know how much you have matured overseas (though they may soon get a good idea). Finding it safer under the circumstances to err on the side of caution, they are likely to treat you the way they did before you left and/or the way they treated your brother or sister at the same age. They get involved in aspects of your life you've had all to yourself for months now, giving advice you feel you have outgrown. They second-guess decisions you've been making on your own since you first arrived in Belgium or Caracas. They want to know about things you haven't shared with adults for some time. They criticize new behaviors you have taken on and lament the passing of certain cherished old behaviors—like listening to and agreeing with them. They ask you how you can like a certain shirt or blouse, how you can not like to do things you used to love doing, and what exactly is wrong with the cooking that used to be good enough for you. In short, they treat you as if you were the same person who went overseas those many months ago—and they can't help doing so because they haven't been a part of your experience.

After having just had the growth experience of a lifetime, for you to be treated as if you had never left home is a nightmare come true. It's not just that such treatment is annoying or demeaning (though it is both) but that it actually undermines the maturity and self-confidence that are probably the greatest and most important legacies of an overseas experience. Indeed, a study of German and American exchange students by David Bachner has shown that a "desire for increased independence" is the most common reason given by students for wanting to go abroad. Now, suddenly, the whole rationale of the adventure seems threatened. "My parents had to realize I had changed," one New Zealand returnee observes, "and that the daughter living with them was not the same submissive person as before. We all had to learn to give and take." Another returning exchangee felt the same way: "Putting up with role expectations from our own parents was very difficult after two years [of] freedom."

Lack of Validation

A related frustration many returning students face is the inability of their parents to understand and appreciate what the overseas experience was like and what it has meant to these students. While research has shown that parents are more interested than either siblings or friends in the overseas experience of their children, there is still a limit to how much they can understand or appreciate. We have chronicled the problem of uninterested compatriots elsewhere in these pages, but in the case of the exchange student this issue takes on added significance because it is one's parents who do not understand.

It is one thing for a grandmother, an uncle, or a best friend not to understand or be interested in one of the seminal experiences of one's life, but it is quite another for one's parents not to be able to relate fully. Young people, especially adolescents, derive much of their self-respect and confidence from the approval and encouragement of others, particularly their parents. To the extent that parents do not or cannot grasp what the overseas experience has been like for the child, the child can expect little validation of that experience from the parent. That is, although the parents may be enthusiastic and deeply proud of what the child has accomplished (as most parents are), the child, knowing the parents haven't entirely understood the nature of the accomplishment, may not derive much comfort from the parents, even if they are saying all the right things. (The children of parents who have lived overseas are likely to be spared this particular frustration.) Not getting the validation they need—or, more accurately, not entirely trusting the validation they receive—exchangees do not automatically get that boost in self-respect and self-confidence that is essential for the creation of an independent identity.

142

If teenagers already had such an identity, none of this would matter much. After all, adult returnees regularly encounter the same lack of understanding and validation from loved ones and more or less take it in stride (apart from the normal disappointment), in large part because they are quite secure in who they are. Teenagers, however, enjoy no such security; indeed, far from being secure in who they are, they are in the midst of creating whoever they are going to be. And to have their self-confidence threatened at such a vulnerable moment can be a deeply troubling experience.

Unflattering Comparisons

The complications of reentering the family sometimes make returnees wish they were back overseas. This sentiment, natural enough under the circumstances, becomes yet another reentry issue once parents get wind of it and begin to suspect that you may actually prefer your host family and overseas life to your natural family and life back home. While this is not entirely the case—most days, anyway—you can't blame your parents for thinking this as you walk around the house carrying on about how fascinating Amsterdam or Chicago was, how wonderful the host family was, how good the host mother's cooking was, what a great tennis player the host father was, and generally what a great time you had abroad. You may not mean anything by all this, but you will have to excuse your family for thinking that you do—for concluding that your life back home can't possibly measure up to the wonders of Paris or Tokyo, that you must therefore be disappointed being home, and that somehow parents and others are a part of this disappointment. In some cases parents may become defensive about themselves and the home culture.

"You want to tell people about [your experience]," an Australian returnee notes, "but sometimes they're jealous, so you can't talk to them. Mum and Dad were jealous of my host parents because I got along so well with them. Sometimes Mum would put them down, which made me really upset."

Shouldering Your Load

Another nasty reentry surprise is the need for the returnee to once again take up household and family responsibilities. In many cases host families treat exchange students more like guests than family members and do not expect of them the kind of participation in the life of the family and running of the household that they expect of their own children or that the exchangees' parents expect of them back home. In some ways a year abroad is a vacation from family obligations and, to a certain extent, from personal responsibility.

When you come home, you are expected to carry your own weight again. This means everything from taking out the garbage and mowing the lawn to helping siblings with homework, taking the car for its tune-up, baby-sitting, visiting Grandfather every Sunday afternoon, and getting a part-time job to earn serious pocket money—none of which may have been a regular part of your exchange experience. Returnees often forget what it was like to be a member of a family and may initially resent what they regard as restrictions on their freedom.

Siblings

Parents aren't the only family members one returns to, of course; there are also brothers and sisters. While siblings, like parents, are happy to see you again, there's no denying that incorporating another person, however beloved, back into a household is bound to be disruptive. On a practical level siblings may have to move out of a cherished room or share that or another room with someone else. The bathroom now also has to be shared with one more person (you) as well as a long list of other items your brothers or sisters may have gotten used to having to themselves, such as a closet, telephone, car, and all manner of personal possessions. "There were certain items in the family," one returnee wrote,

> that had always been everyone's, such as the TV, computer, stereo, etc. However, when I [came] home…my brothers and sisters would have a hard time sharing these things with me because they didn't seem to consider me to be a full-fledged member of the family any longer.

On another level, siblings may resent having to share your parents' attention with you when they have had it all to themselves for the last few months or for a year. Moreover, they may feel threatened by you because you have been places and done things that suddenly dwarf anything they may have accomplished. Younger siblings may act out some of these feelings, while older ones may try to trivialize or make fun of your overseas experience.

Peers and School

Returnees come back not only to their family but also to friends and peers. For the most part the issues here are the same as for expat teenagers, but there are a few wrinkles specific to returning exchange students that bear looking into.

For many exchange students, the decision to go overseas is not well received or understood by their peers. Accordingly, when these students return home, they may be especially eager to demonstrate to peers the wisdom of their decision to go abroad. But these peers, like everyone else back home, aren't especially interested in the returnee's overseas experience, and the returnee may thus never get the chance to justify that original dubious decision, to prove how smart it was to become an exchange student. (Expat kids, by contrast, don't normally feel the same pressure to prove themselves because it wasn't their idea to go abroad in the first place.) One study of exchange students showed that returnees had more difficulty relating to their peers and friends than to either their siblings or parents.

There may also be some problems fitting back into the school curriculum. The overseas school may not have offered certain courses that are required for graduation or are prerequisites for other courses you need or want to take. The home school may not give credit for some courses taken overseas, and you may have missed important local or national exams and have to scramble to make them up.

The Loss of Language

Unlike expat kids, for whom learning a foreign language is just part of the fun of being overseas, for exchange and study abroad students, learning a language is often a major reason for going overseas in the first place. Consequently, mastering and speaking that language becomes a major focus of the overseas sojourn and an important part of the returnee's new identity.

Small wonder, then, that the return of these students and the resulting loss (or fear of loss) of the foreign language can be profoundly upsetting. It feels like an assault on their identity, and they fight back mightily, insisting on speaking Swedish or Hindi to their parents and other astonished monolinguals. But they have to know it's a losing battle. With their identity already under attack from other quarters, the loss of language is just more salt on already open wounds.

No Longer a Celebrity

High school exchange students tend to stand out in their overseas school and in the local community. More often than not, they are the only Italian or Brazilian or American for miles around, which naturally makes them feel rather special. They may be much sought after as friends or to give talks or presentations. They may be interviewed by the local newspaper or TV station. Wherever they go, they become the center of attention and the object of considerable interest and speculation. While their novelty value wears off after a while, exchange students find that in the beginning almost everything they say and do seems noteworthy.

Coming home isn't quite like that. There's a flurry of excitement in the beginning, of course, when you appear on the scene once again after months of absence, creating quite a stir the first time you visit Grandma, your high school, and the local teen hangout. But you are absorbed back into the fabric of people's lives with remarkable—and disappointing—speed. And you don't stand out to strangers the way you did overseas. Suddenly, you're anonymous; you feel almost invisible. The contrast, after being a minor sensation abroad, is so striking as to be almost visceral.

Homesickness

While all returning teenagers miss those people with whom they have formed close relationships overseas, returning exchange students are especially vulnerable on this account, for they have typically formed much closer ties than has the average expatriate.

This is because the exchangee lives with a host family and inevitably becomes close to host parents and siblings. It is one thing to leave a friend behind, someone seen regularly at school, but it is quite another to leave behind a host father and mother and host brother and sister, people whose home and whose lives you have shared day in and day out for many months. "I cried for two months," an exchangee from Ecuador remembered. "I just loved my American family. I think about [them] every day."

Returning Alone

The sting of reentry, as we've noted before, is made worse by the fact that no one understands what you are going through. Indeed, most people can't even imagine what there is to go through. While expat students are not spared this pain either, they at least have the advantage of returning with their parents and siblings, who do understand (to some extent, anyway) their discomfort. But you don't have this luxury; instead of being sources of support during reentry, your parents are often a large part of the problem. In any event, as lonely as the return can be for teenagers in general, it can be even lonelier for returning exchange students.

147

The End of the Adventure

Bachner's study, cited earlier, found that the other key motive exchangees gave for wanting to go overseas was to satisfy a sense of adventure. To the extent that reentry signals the end of that adventure, it becomes another issue for exchangees to deal with. While this notion has been discussed in chapter 1, it is mentioned again here only to stress that the end of the adventure—of a period of intense personal growth and stimulation—may be more deeply felt by exchangees, since the search for that kind of experience was so much a part of their reason for going abroad in the first place. This may not be the case for returning expat students, who won't necessarily have had this (or any) motive for going overseas, though they may very well have appreciated the adventure once it fell into their lap.

What Exchange Students and Their Families Can Do

While most of the important strategies for reentry were covered at the end of chapters 1 and 3, a few words of additional advice are offered here. Returning exchange students should be especially careful to say proper good-byes to host family members and to patch up any quarrels before they depart. Exchangees and host families become close, and everyone concerned will want to end this experience on a positive note.

You and your family should make every effort to be as patient with each other as possible. You have not lived together for several months (or a year), and it is bound to take some time to be comfortable with each other. You should also be very patient with yourself during reentry, whether you are a family member or the exchangee, and not think something is wrong with you because this reunion is not going as well as you expected.

Exchangees should be careful not to compare their family and their home culture unfavorably with their host family and culture, at least not out loud. While it's only natural to find you prefer many things about your overseas life to your life back home, your parents may not understand this. Save these unflattering comparisons for the times you are together with other returnees like yourself.

When you get home, you should be sure to ask friends and family members about what has happened in their lives while you were abroad. "My family loved to hear me talk about the experience," a Swedish exchangee observed, "but they also thought I demanded too much attention and that I forgot to take part in what had happened to them during the year."

Exchangees and their families should talk about some of the adjustments they are going through and problems they are having. While talking doesn't make the issues go away, it can neutralize some of them and can also keep tension from building.

More than other returning teens, exchangees should find other study abroad returnees to talk with about reentry. Returning expatriate families at least have other family members to talk to and commiserate with, but exchangees don't have anyone. At the same time, the parents of returnees can find solace, even wisdom, in talking to other parents who have received sojourners back into the bosom of the family.

During the worst moments of reentry, exchangees may need a lifeline to their host family and overseas friends, the most effective of which is the freedom to make lengthy, expensive international phone calls. Exchangees need to know they belong and are accepted somewhere. As long as they do not feel altogether at ease or accepted in their natural family and home culture, then feeling a part of their host family and overseas culture is a great source of comfort and reassurance. Paradoxically, knowing that they are still accepted overseas makes it possible for exchangees to begin to fit in back home.

149

Another comfort for you is the chance to maintain some kind of exposure to the overseas culture and language. It may be possible to take an advanced class or listen to radio or TV programs in that language. Maybe there are people from that country, perhaps students your own age, in the town or area where you live. Your family may be able to host an exchange student from abroad or put up international visitors, or your school may have one or more foreign exchange students you can befriend. If it's not possible to have continued contact with the same culture you lived in overseas, you may at least be able to have contact with students from other countries or with other young people from your country who were also exchange students (many countries have national alumni groups) and who share some of your values and interests.

You can give slide shows and make other presentations at your school or to local civic groups.

Finally, as you readjust, think back to your initial adjustment overseas. Remember how you were homesick then, too, how you doubted that you would ever get used to that place, and wondered if you had made a mistake in going abroad. Then, slowly, your feelings began to change, and you became more at ease and content in the new country. This will happen back home also, if you give yourself time. "I am pained at my vague, bitter nostalgia for all that I knew," one returnee notes, "but I know that here, in the near future, I can be happy, as long as I learn to cope with change and believe [that everything will work out] in time."

Meanwhile, during the worst moments of reentry, try not to lose sight of what the overseas experience has meant to you and how much it has changed you for the better. You wouldn't really change anything, would you, even if you could? "I've experienced different cultures, traditions, views of life," an American returning from Africa wrote. "I feel I am a more accepting and open-minded person because of my experiences. I have access to the best of both worlds now: the openness, freedom, and opportunity of America and the diversity, warmth, and beauty of Africa."

II. International Voluntary Organizations

The contrast between the relaxed way I lived in Tonga and the rushing, stark, blank faces and buildings and way of life was so marked that the day I arrived home I could hardly stand it.

—Returned New Zealand volunteer

The Issues

For years a number of countries have sent (mainly) young people to developing nations to work as volunteers for one or two years. The United Kingdom has its VSO (Volunteers in Service Overseas), Canada has CUSO (Canadian University Students Overseas), Japan has JOCV (Japanese Overseas Corps of Volunteers), and the United States has its Peace Corps, to name just a few. Volunteers returning from these assignments are no more immune to the readjustment blues than are any other population and, indeed, typically go through an especially intense reentry. In a 1996 Peace Corps study, for example, 56 percent of returning volunteers said they found their return "somewhat" or "very" difficult.

The Volunteer Lifestyle

Most of the special issues returning volunteers face derive from the somewhat unique way they spend their two or more years abroad. The basic service concept of many international volunteer agencies is that volunteers work directly with (and under) host country people and live cheek by jowl with them. Volunteers are typically assigned to host organizations or institutions, whether government or private, where they are usually the only national from their country and where they accordingly have to learn and conform to the cultural norms of the workplace. Outside of work, volunteers live in the local culture and once again must learn and conform to many of the norms and behaviors expected of people in that society. Their houses, meanwhile, may not have electricity or running water, or they may not have a house at all but live instead with local families.

To be effective, then, volunteers must become deeply immersed in the lives of the local people and must try to understand their view of the world. In the process volunteers often adopt many of the local norms and behaviors and begin to identify more closely with the host country way of life. While they do not become host country nationals, of course, neither do they remain entirely natives of their home country.

Needless to say, for these volunteers the foreign culture becomes home in a much more profound way than it does for the typical expatriate, who normally lives much more on the periphery of the local culture. And the readjustment to their real home, therefore, is likewise much more intense. Whereas businesspeople report taking an average of six months to readjust, nearly one-third of the Peace Corps volunteers studied between 1968 and 1996 said it took them more than a year to readjust. "I don't know about the rest of you volunteers," one returnee wrote recently on the Internet, "but I still [get nervous] drawing water from a tap. It has only been twenty-five years since my return."

Two other features distinguish how international volunteers spend their time abroad: the countries they serve in and the posts they are assigned to within those countries. By and large volunteers serve in developing countries (over half of all American volunteers, for example, work in Africa) and are typically posted outside of the major cities, in towns and villages—places where the need for technical assistance is the greatest. Many volunteers, as a result, adjust to and lead relatively simple lives, doing without what they hitherto regarded as essentials—things like running water, electricity (and the appliances that depend on it), telephones, regular and reliable transportation, all manner of material goods, and in some cases (and some seasons) all but the most basic food. While many of these adjustments are in fact easier than they sound—most volunteers will tell you that the real hardships overseas are of the emotional and psychological kind—taking on this lifestyle makes a deep and lasting impression. Many volunteers come to prefer this simpler, slower-paced life, feeling more and more liberated as the list of life's necessities gets ever shorter and the list of luxuries ever longer.

When these people come home, there are some problems, starting usually at the supermarket—actually larger, in some cases, than the entire village the volunteer just came from—where their homeland's great abundance is laid out, aisle after aisle, in all its glory. "Going into the supermarket was an embarrassment," a volunteer who had served in Ghana remembers, "seeing seventy kinds of dog food. I mean they're just *dogs*; they'll eat anything!" Another returnee recalled that in his village "there were times when all we had to eat was millet. Even if you could afford something else, that's all there was. I tried the [pharmacy] when I first got home, but I only made it down two aisles. I still can't handle the mall."

153

Difficult as it is to adjust to the abundance, waste, and excess of material comforts, many volunteers have an even harder time adjusting to the attitude of their compatriots who don't seem to appreciate what they have. "How can Americans be so rich—and so discontented?" a volunteer who had returned from Malawi asks. "I took a three-day bus trip across the country," another returnee recalls, "and I couldn't believe how comfortable the bus was. But everyone else was really agitated; they were always complaining about something. I mean, this bus had air conditioning and a bathroom, right there on the bus!"

The pace of life is another challenge. "People are so busy back home," a returned volunteer observed. "There's so much coming at you. People don't sit and talk. No one really listens. What I miss most about Africa is sitting on the porch in the evening cracking peanuts. Try doing that here!" One can talk to more people and do more things in a single day in one's home country than in a week or a month in some overseas sites. "I wanted to reduce all the noise that was coming in," a volunteer having returned from Eastern Europe recalls. "I stayed in my room for five days without coming out."

Some volunteers struggle with how narrow and superficial the interests and concerns of many of their compatriots are. Volunteers get caught up, many of them, in some of the great issues of the times—poverty, political oppression—only to find friends and family neither aware of nor interested in some of these matters. "When I arrived back, I felt completely alienated from the values in New Zealand" one returnee remembers. "[The] society was concerned with such shallow [things] while other people were starving. I tried to talk about all this, but I was either treated with indifference or told what a silly thing it was to have volunteered."

Returning volunteers not only dislike much of what they see back home, they are deeply threatened by it. They see readjusting to their home country as abandoning not merely the simpler lifestyle they became accustomed to overseas but more importantly the stronger, freer, healthier person they have become as a result of living so simply. To these people, readjustment is not merely uncomfortable but something to be actively fought, a struggle to preserve one's identity. While other returnees may have some ambivalence about readjustment, few of them struggle with it as intensely as returning volunteers.

Feeling as they do, many returnees strongly resist reintegrating into society. Oh, they eat the sushi or the ice cream (worried, as ever, about amoebas) and somehow manage to cope with indoor plumbing, but they consciously eschew many of the luxuries—not to mention the necessities—of life back home. Television, with its multiple channels, goes untouched for months, years in some cases. Air conditioning is certainly not necessary, as is the case with many other items that have the fatal flaw of being electric, such as food processors, dishwashers, and can openers. Deodorant and perfume are looked down upon. Beds may likewise be suspect, when a mattress on the floor will do nicely. Nor do rooms necessarily need furniture. Buses are good enough, even if there is a plane going to the same place for almost the same price.

"I'm afraid I may be becoming readjusted," a returnee observes, agreeing with another returnee who worries that "readjusting would take me back to what I was before. I think of it as being back in the mainstream grind. I want life to be slower paced. It helps me remember what I lived like overseas. I don't think I'll ever totally readjust. At least I hope I don't."

Losing Your Language

Another important dimension of the international volunteer experience with a direct bearing upon reentry is the fact that most volunteers become proficient in a foreign language; for them mastering and especially functioning in another language is an exhilarating experience. Every day there is a small linguistic triumph: using the past tense correctly for the first time, finally understanding a phrase they've heard over and over and never quite grasped, using that phrase themselves a few weeks later, completing an entire transaction at the bank or the post office having understood everything that was said, making their first joke, their first play on words, successfully eavesdropping, and so on.

Watching yourself confront and overcome these challenges is an immensely satisfying experience and a great boost to your self-esteem. For volunteers from English-speaking countries, there is also a great deal of pleasure to be had from seeing how thrilled and shocked people are that a native English speaker has learned their language (especially if theirs is not one of the international languages).

Now, back home, with your new language of no use to you, that exhilaration and satisfaction are gone. No more creating a

155

sensation when you walk into a shop in Morocco or Tunisia and ask for sugar in perfect Arabic. No one thinks it's quaint that you speak English (though they may think your English is quaint). Speaking used to make you feel special; now it just makes you miss living overseas. "Polish is such a beautiful language," one returnee recalled. "I spoke 100 percent of the time in Polish. When I got back home there was no opportunity to speak it. It was so annoying to feel my skills slipping away."

The lack of opportunity isn't a problem for all returned volunteers, however. "I used to slip into Swahili when I first got back," a volunteer who returned from Kenya remembers, "and get these blank stares. But there are some things you just can't translate. There's this great curse—'Your mother was a chicken so you had to suckle a cow'—but it doesn't really sound that bad in English."

Cut Loose

Another adjustment some returning volunteers have to make is no longer being a part of the VSO/CUSO/Peace Corps organization. Whether one hates it or loves it, the agency bureaucracy looms large in a volunteer's life overseas. It takes complete care of many of their basic needs (health care, mail, professional development), troubleshoots in a number of other areas (housing problems, problems at work, family emergencies back home), reimburses all manner of expenses—and also dictates a fair amount of volunteers' behavior. This concern about your welfare is considerably more than an employer provides and just short of a second set of parents. While you may have grumbled about being treated like a child at times or otherwise resented the organization's intrusion into your personal and professional life, you most likely identified closely with the organization and regularly relied on it in times of need.

And now it's gone. Suddenly there's no one to run interference for you; no one who takes complete responsibility for your medical care, reminding you to come in for your gamma globulin shot and sending you medications when you run out; no one who sends you a duplicate check when someone steals your living allowance; no one who cables your mother to say you're okay when you don't write for months.

Work—and Meaningful Work

Returning volunteers must also come to terms with being unemployed and having to look for a job. Unlike most returning adult sojourners, former volunteers typically have no work waiting for them upon reentry. While many returnees, as we have seen, don't think much of the position they get upon reentry, at least they *have* a position, and for all their legitimate complaints, most would probably not trade their job for a stint of unemployment.

157

Adjusting to unemployment, difficult under the best of circumstances, is especially traumatic for many volunteers because of the kind of jobs they had overseas. Most volunteers serve in responsible positions with considerable authority and influence, especially for their age, and are used to being respected (if not always listened to). Many are teachers in cultures where teachers are highly respected and deferred to, and others serve as civil servants in the government in cultures where a bureaucrat is virtually a lesser god. For volunteers in many countries, simply being college-educated automatically makes them members of an elite, people of genuine substance. The fall from a person of substance to unemployment can be a breathtaking plunge.

For some returnees landing a job, no matter how good, may not be the answer to quite all of their prayers. A volunteer who brought running water to a remote village in Nepal or ran a malaria-eradication program in Cameroon may not find working in an accounting firm all that satisfying. Because of the scale of the needs in many developing countries, volunteers often find themselves in jobs that have a profound, and sometimes immediate, impact on people's lives. Even volunteers in the education sector, where the impact of their efforts may be more indirect and long-term, very often teach children who would otherwise not have a teacher at all. Back home, it's hard to find work quite this worthwhile. "My job consisted of sitting at a desk in a large room," one returnee remembered,

> *where several other men spent most of the day drinking coffee and chatting with one another. When I asked for something to do, I was told to take a coffee break. After about a week of this, I begged the supervisor to give me something—anything—to do. He finally brought me a large book, a rubber stamp, and an ink pad and proceeded for about ten minutes to show me how to press the rubber stamp to the ink pad and then to stamp each line on each page with this single stamp. After about half an hour I was told to slow down my pace by one of my coworkers.... I only lasted four weeks on that job, and that was because I gave two weeks' notice.*

158

What Returning Volunteers Can Do

There is little in the way of unique advice to offer here; the suggestions given at the end of chapter 1 should prove to be good therapy for what ails most returning volunteers. As we noted earlier, you will probably want to give yourself more time to readjust than typical expatriates, and you should also take special care not to be too hard on your compatriots or your home country. After all, you used to like these people and this place, so you can probably learn to do so again, if you're patient. And patience, God knows, is one thing you surely must have learned when you were overseas.

Looking for work, especially in the era of downsizing and corporate reengineering—better known as layoffs—can be a frustrating and lengthy proposition. You may find it easier to settle initially for something less than the perfect job, so you can at least pay your bills; then use that position as a base for your ongoing search. You should also be aware that many stateside employers aren't going to understand what your overseas volunteer job was all about. They're not going to know, unless you tell them, what kind of skills and expertise it left you with or what it might qualify you for.

Seeking out other former volunteers is also important, for all the usual reasons, but especially to verify that you aren't the only one eating with your hands in fancy restaurants and hanging your laundry on the front hedge to dry.

In the end you will readjust, of course, not in the sense that your overseas experience will fade from your consciousness, but to the extent that you will find a way to incorporate the best parts of that experience into your life back home. There are, incidentally, telltale signs of returning volunteer readjustment (see Figure 5.1); if you exhibit five or more of these behaviors, there's probably no turning back for you.

Figure 5.1
Ten Ways International Volunteers
Know They Have Readjusted

1. You've stopped carrying toilet paper with you wherever you go.
2. You no longer eat all the hors d'oeuvres at dinner parties.
3. Some of your clothes are not out of date.
4. Other people no longer avoid the dish you bring to potluck dinners.

Figure 5.1 (cont.)

5. You have a friend who was never an international volunteer.
6. You occasionally stay in a hotel when you are in a strange city.
7. You dream in your native language.
8. You use tissues to blow your nose.
9. You occasionally use public transportation instead of walking.
10. You're not afraid to swallow water while showering.

III. Military Personnel and Their Families

I felt lost.... The Army seems to care more about families overseas than at home. Overseas, I felt more informed about what was happening. In the States, I feel out of it all the time.

—U.S. Army spouse

While it is risky to generalize about any of the populations in this chapter, we venture even further out on our limb in this section. For one thing many countries that post military personnel abroad may have several major service branches, each with its own separate reality and set of issues; then within each branch there is also diversity: between officers and enlisted men, between those making a career of the military and those passing through, between those who go overseas with their families (usually called an accompanied tour) and return together and those on unaccompanied tours, and between those who live on base overseas and those who do not. We remain undaunted by our task, but we do apologize to those service men and women and their families who may not recognize themselves in this section.

Most married service men and women take their families with them when they are posted abroad, except in times of war or when the service member is being sent to a place where the risks to dependents are too great or the living conditions inadequate. These families return and go through reentry together, much like the typical expatriate discussed in earlier chapters. While such accompanied tours are the norm in the military, unaccompanied tours are also fairly common, where the service member leaves his or her spouse and children behind and returns to them several months later. Unaccompanied tours are common in the navy—whenever a ship or submarine leaves its base, almost everyone on board is unaccompanied for the duration of the deployment. While months-long unaccompanied tours are relatively rare in the army and air force, most branches of the military have shorter unaccompanied tours, lasting three to four weeks, where the service member is usually on some kind of special assignment. Needless to say, reentry from an accompanied and an unaccompanied tour will be quite different, and we will, therefore, take up each one separately.

161

The Issues

Accompanied Tours

As a rule, military families move far more often than their counterparts in the general population and are therefore likely to be more adept than civilians at dealing with many of the issues associated with relocation. Even so, reentry hits them as hard as it does the typical expatriate and, more importantly, hits them in ways not experienced by other expatriates.

Whatever branch of service you belong to, chances are the government took good care of you and your families overseas. Whether you lived on or off a military base during an accompanied tour, the base was no doubt a major focus of your life. American military families, for example, usually shop at the base commissary, go to the base library for books, and to the base gym, child development center, cinema, and church. Beyond that, the military probably looked after your medical and dental needs, helped out in times of family emergencies, paid your speeding tickets, and lent a hand when a son or daughter was picked up for disorderly conduct. Needless to say, you adjusted quite nicely to this kind of care.

Similarly, you sorely miss it when the rug is pulled out from under you back home, where the military is typically not prepared to deliver this kind of support. This is your own country, after all; you should be able to manage on your own. And by and large people do, but not without a struggle. "We were out of practice living in a nonmilitary world," one spouse remembered. "We didn't speak civilian, and no one oriented us to the local community the way we were oriented to the base [when we went abroad.]" The adjustment is no doubt greater for those who return to large metropolitan areas than for those who return to smaller base towns, but even in base towns, the level of support from the military does not compare favorably with what was available abroad.

A related adjustment facing most military returnees is the loss of community and with it, part of one's identity. Life on or near an overseas military base is a family affair, no matter how large the facility. Sharing this rich, intense experience of living thousands of miles from home and extended family and surrounded by an unfamiliar culture, most military personnel and their families feel a bond with other military personnel, whether they've ever met or not. "We're all part of the family," one spouse observes. "No one in a commissary on any base in the world would hesitate to ask anyone else in that commissary where something is. I defy you to find that in any civilian grocery store." Among the overseas military, another spouse notes, "You become very interdependent. You *must* become interdependent. Your closest friends in life are the ones [you] meet overseas."

Unless you resettle in a small base town, coming home is a return to relative isolation and anonymity. The ready-made community you belonged to overseas (whether you wanted to or not) is gone. The only community you will have now is the one you make for yourself, with considerable effort. "You feel a tremendous sense of loss," one returnee remembers, "of self and identity. You're a nameless, faceless person lost in a sea of nameless, faceless people."

Many families, especially those posted to large urban areas, have a hard time settling permanently, moving two or three times before they end up in the neighborhood or suburb that is right for them. Because they have never lived in this city before, they don't know enough to make intelligent choices about where to buy a house. You may discover, for example, that the schools in your area aren't what you want for your children or that you have ended up with a dreadful commute or that your neighborhood isn't safe. Along with all the other challenges of reentry, having to move again a few months after you have "settled in" is the last straw.

Another common concern for returning military families is discipline problems with their children. Overseas, life is lived in something of a fishbowl; most people know most other people's business, and anonymity is a precious commodity. In that environment, children feel under more than the usual pressure to behave themselves. As if that weren't enough, children are under the added pressure of knowing that if they act up, they and one of their parents will be sent home while the other parent stays on to finish his or her tour. Few teenagers or preteens want to be responsible for that particular burden.

When these children return to the relative anonymity of life back home, especially in large urban and suburban locations, much of the pressure to be the model child is gone—and there is lost time to make up for. Now you may discover that your children are not the perfect sons or daughters you had thought they were.

Most military families are shocked at the cost of reentry. This is true of most returnees, as we noted earlier, but in the case of

163

the military the problem is that returnees may have been told the government will cover the costs of their move. While this is true for U.S. military personnel, there are many costs associated with moving that Uncle Sam does not pay for. A recent U.S. Air Force study found that on the average returnees pay 35 percent of all moving costs out of their own pocket. It's one thing to be surprised at the costs of reentry but quite another to believe that those costs were being paid for only to discover that many of them are not. There is no intent to mislead here on the part of the military; the problem, usually, is that many families do not educate themselves well enough on relocation policies.

In today's military, some spouses choose not to accompany the service member overseas, unwilling to interrupt a promising career, for example, or to take the children out of high school. This then becomes an unaccompanied tour.

Unaccompanied Tours

In many military organizations, unaccompanied tours of five to twelve months' duration are not uncommon (not in the U.S. Navy or Marine Corps, anyway, though they are still the exception in the U.S. Army; that may change, however, in today's world, when the Army is being used increasingly for peacekeeping and humanitarian missions). Reentry from an unaccompanied tour is so unlike that from an accompanied tour that the Navy doesn't use the word *reentry*, preferring *reunion* instead. While reunion—the return of the service member to his or her spouse and children—is no doubt the most important aspect of the return from an unaccompanied tour, we should note for the record that the returnee also goes through reentry, whether the Navy uses the word or not. Reunion, in short, is really just one more reentry issue, albeit a crucial one, which deserves our close attention.

But we're getting ahead of ourselves. Before the reunion comes the separation, the period of prolonged absence of the service man (it is almost always a man in the U.S. Navy and the Marines), during which time a great deal happens, both at home to the spouse and children and abroad to the service man. Needless to say, the lives the two halves of the family lead during the separation have great consequences for the reunion.

Daily life for the service man is still lived for the most part in an all-male environment, where some of the norms are rough language and bawdy stories, macho behavior and sexist attitudes. And he gets into the habit of being responsible only for himself. The service is also a regimented environment, with very clear lines of authority and a somewhat limited range of interpersonal interactions. It is a comparatively static existence, monotonous, and all in all not very good practice for life in the civilian world.

While the seaman has been living in and adjusting to this world, you, his spouse, have typically undergone something of a transformation. Whether you like it or not, you are now the sole parent, de facto head of the family, obliged to be both mother and father. While you may be able to consult your husband on a regular basis, the real burden of most decisions falls squarely on you. You know the context, after all, the things that have happened since your husband left, and while his input may be useful, you can't possibly educate him enough over the telephone or through e-mail to be able to trust his advice as much as you trust your own instincts. With young families there are scores of such decisions, everything from whether to get braces for the children to whether the youngest son should sign up for soccer or baseball to whether to change the oldest daughter's doctor. This is complicated by the fact that, of course, these are not merely your children but your husband's too, adding to the pressure to do things right. Moreover, there may be times when you cannot communicate with your husband—when he is on a submarine, for example, or on a ship far from shore.

You rise to the occasion, out of necessity, normally becoming quite independent and self-sufficient in the process. And children also adjust to the new family dynamic, helping out more around the home, perhaps, and generally taking on the absent father's duties where possible. Indeed, many fathers enjoin their sons to look after Mother while he is away, telling them, "You're the man of the house now."

What happens, then, when you, the real "man of the house" return? From your point of view, the sudden return to a coed environment calls for some attitude and behavior adjustment. You must clean up your speech or else, and you put women down at your peril. You have to learn again how to put the needs of others before your own or at least on the same level as your own, and you have to learn how to behave in all manner of settings that you may not have been in for months, such as dinner parties, church services, school meetings, shopping in a supermarket, going to a film at a suburban cineplex, or simply being in a mixed group of men and women. You have to figure out how to live with a wife and children who have managed without you. It should be noted here that in many ways the environment the husband has been in has reinforced the more traditional—some would say sexist—view of women in society, even as the situation the wife has been put in has obliged her to take on nontraditional roles.

You, the wife, meanwhile, also have to learn how to live with a partner again. Suddenly, you have to consult with your husband on decisions that by now have become second nature to you and to share responsibilities you have had all to yourself for months. Having mastered the roles of mother *and* father, you now have to cede the latter to the genuine article. Many wives are more than happy to oblige, of course, but others may think they filled the role rather better than their husbands do.

Now is the time the husband will confront the reality of the many decisions his wife has had to make in his absence, and unless he is an unusual man, he is certain to take issue with some of them. His wife, meanwhile, won't appreciate being second-guessed, especially since it wasn't her idea to have to run the family by herself anyway. The biggest trouble spot here, typically, is the matter of disciplining the children. Inevitably, the wife will have charted a stricter or more lenient course than the husband would have in certain areas, and now the absent spouse weighs in with his midcourse corrections. If the parents are wise, they will have this conflict behind closed doors and visit the carefully worked-out results upon the children in a united front. If the spouses aren't thinking, the returnee will confront the children directly with the new realities and thereby undermine his wife's credibility as an authority figure. Whichever way it falls out, dealing with this issue is almost never pleasant.

The children must adjust to the new family dynamics also. Their mother, as noted above, is suddenly no longer the final authority on family matters. Meanwhile, the son who was told he was the man of the family and has adjusted quite well to his adult responsibilities now has to revert to being a child again. Children who have been the center of their mother's universe must now share her attention with their father; sometimes they are even packed off to the grandparents for a visit so Mom and Dad can be alone. Duties assumed by the children in the father's absence now have to be diplomatically redistributed.

Absent Wives

While husbands still make up the majority of service members on unaccompanied tours, the military is becoming an increasingly coed institution. Both Desert Storm and Bosnia have seen the deployment of female spouses from a number of countries whose husbands stayed behind to manage the family. Absent wives make for a much different family dynamic than absent husbands do and create different reentry issues. Children generally feel more abandoned when their mother leaves and may be resentful and hard to win over when she returns. As a rule, husbands have a much harder time adjusting to being the sole parent and typically involve grand-parents much more in the everyday life of the family. These same grandparents, used to being key players, may have a hard time bowing out when their daughter or daughter-in-law returns. Fa-thers, meanwhile, have to adjust to being one of two parents again and may miss the closeness they established with their children.

Shorter Assignments

Another type of unaccompanied tour, common to all the service branches, is a short, three- to six-week assignment. For some ser-vice members, these assignments are isolated—one every year or two, and relatively easy to manage. But for others, they occur every two or three months. While the return from these assign-ments is technically not reentry, in the sense that the individual has not been abroad long enough to have settled into the overseas location and lifestyle, it often raises some reentry-like havoc, es-pecially with regard to certain of the reunion issues discussed above. Probably the greatest concern is determining the exact sta-tus of the service member who keeps dropping in and out of the family. Is this person a visitor, to be treated one way, or a bona fide parent, to be treated quite another? Does the at-home spouse make important decisions in the interim periods or wait? And does the at-home spouse have to be consistent about this, always mak-ing decisions or always waiting? Many military spouses find these short assignments, when they occur in succession, harder to man-age than reunion after the classic unaccompanied tour.

The Culture of Keeping Quiet

For service members and their families, reentry is further compli-cated by the tradition in the military of being tough, which ap-plies both to those in uniform and to their dependents, especially spouses. The notion is that one rolls with the punches and doesn't complain, much less ask for help. The safest strategy is to deny that one is having problems, in this case with reentry. "Denial is part of the military culture," one returnee notes. "So we don't express reentry feelings, or people will think we're just weak. The spouse is especially pressured to be a good trooper." And the military spouse, as we have noted elsewhere, is often having a harder time than the service member, who at least has a ready-made identity waiting for him or her. The Navy's attitude in general toward the family of the service member has been famously summed up in what is called the "seabag mentality": "If they'd wanted you to have a family, they would have issued you one in your seabag." (To be fair, we should also note that in the United States the Navy leads the other branches in research in and workshops on reentry.)

169

What Military Returnees and Their Families Can Do

Families returning from accompanied tours should not be afraid to ask for help with their reentry problems. In the United States several organizations exist within the military to assist individuals during this difficult transition, including the National Military Family Association and the Department of Defense Relocation Assistance Program (with a relocation office for each service branch). The latter offers numerous workshops in the whole range of reentry concerns. Families should also educate themselves on the fine print of relocation policies so there will be fewer surprises regarding which costs associated with moving are and which are not covered by the government.

You should realize that you have been set up, in a way, by the considerable support you received from the military when you were abroad, and you should give yourself plenty of time to get used to being on your own back home. At the very least, do not be too hard on yourself, wondering what's wrong with you when you seem unable to cope back in your own country. What's wrong is that you became quite accustomed to being taken care of and are now a little out of practice.

As far as possible, you should collect information on the new place you are being posted to, so you can make a better choice about where to live and not have to move again three months after you have settled in. This information is usually available overseas, and you can also talk to families at post who have lived in these cities.

The best preparation for returning from an unaccompanied tour is for the service member to have as much contact with family members as possible while abroad so as not to be forgotten or to be a stranger upon reentry. Whether it's frequent e-mails, phone calls, videos, pictures, or long letters, anything that keeps you current on developments back home is bound to ease the strain of reunion. Spouses should be patient with each other during reentry, understanding that neither will be immediately comfortable in this new family dynamic and that it will take time for everyone to sort out roles and responsibilities.

IV. Missionaries and Missionary Children

Right now, I don't have a sense of belonging anywhere. I feel like an outsider. It's not a very pleasant feeling, but with God's help I believe I can live with it.

—Returning missionary

Christian missionaries from all of Europe and North America (not including dependents) are estimated at eighty to ninety thousand. Needless to say, the missionary community is no more monolithic than any of the other communities featured in this chapter. One of the greatest distinctions is the difference between short-term and career missionaries. Short-term missionaries normally serve one time, in one place, usually for fewer than three years, and then resume their lives back home. In many ways the reentry of short-term missionaries is similar to the generic model presented in this book.

Career missionaries, on the other hand, normally spend many years in service, in the same place or in several places, returning periodically on home leave and then going back into the field. While these home leaves or furloughs are, in effect, multiple reentries, home leave differs from classic reentry in one key respect: it is of limited duration, typically from six months to a year, and the missionary knows he or she is going back into the field at the end of the specified time. Most of the issues discussed in this section apply more to career than to short-term missionaries. A few, though, apply to both and are as much home leave issues as they are reentry concerns. We have divided this section into two parts: issues facing missionaries themselves and issues for missionary children.

Issues for Missionaries
The Fruits of One's Labor

One of the most significant issues returning missionaries face is the question of accountability. What did you accomplish while you were overseas? Since the work of missionaries is made possible by the donations of church members back home, there is more than the usual interest in knowing how the money was spent. "There are expectations of high productivity," observes David Pollock, a specialist in missionary adjustment and reentry issues. Specifically, donors want to hear success stories, to feel that their donation, however meager, made all the difference in the lives of countless people in Brazil or Malaysia. In some cases, you can supply these kinds of results, but in many others you cannot. The problem is that results come in different guises; some are imminently observable and measurable, while others are indirect and intangible. Moreover, for some missionaries, the fruits of their labor ripen quickly, but for others they ripen exceedingly slow and often not until long after the missionary has departed. "A guy who starts churches in the slums of São Paulo can have a phenomenal success rate," one observer has noted. "But someone who spends ten years in Beirut may not have that much to show for it." Missionaries know their supporters want this kind of tangible success and often put themselves under great pressure to produce it. When they do not, they can be as disappointed as their sponsors.

What has been called the lone-ranger mentality increases the pressure on missionaries to get results in the field. Missionaries tend to be more independent of their sponsoring organization than expatriates in the private sector or in government, working on their own in many cases and taking more personal responsibility for their work. If they succeed, it is at least in part a personal triumph; if they fail, it is a personal failure.

A related frustration here is figuring out how to explain to your lesser-traveled and relatively unworldly compatriots just what you are up against as you go about doing God's work in Africa or Latin America. Not understanding the context in which you work, sponsors may not be able to appreciate the real value of what you have achieved, especially if the results have not been dramatic.

On the Road

A related problem here is the tremendous pressure put on returning missionaries to travel and tell their stories back home. The success of your efforts, after all, depends on the continuing support of church members in the home country, supporters whose attention needs to be periodically refocused on the urgent tasks at hand. Your so-called furloughs or home leaves may not be spent in relaxation and regeneration but with at least you or your spouse traveling around the country and to neighboring countries for weeks at a time inspiring the faithful. The problem here is the difficulties this travel and the prolonged absence of one parent create for your family. Many missionaries have mixed feelings about home leave for this very reason, knowing family life will be mightily disrupted until everyone is together again back overseas. If home leave were a relaxed, enjoyable time, this aspect of missionary life wouldn't be so traumatic, but home leave, as we are seeing in this section, poses a number of serious challenges for missionaries and their children, challenges which the at-home parent is often left to confront alone.

Money

Money can also be a problem for missionaries on home leave. Contributions often dry up during furlough, with many donors believing that when you are not in the field, you are not doing real mission work. While a number of countries prohibit contributions to individual missionaries, in actual practice many donors often support specific missions and specific individuals.

Judgments and Doubt

Like international volunteers, missionaries typically serve in locations where they may have to live without running water and electricity, adjust to a limited selection of food and other material goods, and rely only on books and conversation for entertainment. For missionaries from any of the wealthy industrialized democracies, reentry can be a shocking lesson in contrasts, being suddenly surrounded by so much comfort, wealth, and abundance—and so much waste. Having adjusted to a much simpler and quieter style and pace of life overseas, you may find the version of life offered back home overwhelming. "The jolt of being plunked back into the middle of affluence," David Pollock has noted in an interview with me, is too much for many missionaries. Like the former volunteers mentioned earlier, missionaries "are just not ready to walk down the dog food aisle and see diet dog food," Pollock continues. "The dissonance of values [between abroad and home] is too great."

Missionaries are sometimes shocked at the general permissiveness of their home culture. In many countries movies, books, and television present increasingly violent and sexually explicit fare, drugs are readily available, and the morals of young people offer quite a contrast to what missionary children are used to in the fishbowl of an overseas post. In the United States children and their parents also worry about the crime and violence in society.

Like most returnees, missionaries react strongly to these phenomena: to the abundance and waste, to the lack of concern for the poor, to the permissiveness and violence, and also to the general provincialism and narrow-mindedness of many of their compatriots. But for missionaries this reaction becomes a serious reentry issue of its own, because they may be unable to reconcile it with their image of themselves as tolerant, caring, nonjudgmental individuals who also happen to be good at crossing cultures. Doubt arises. If I can't love and get along with my own kind, how can I care for and minister to those I work with overseas? To have their self-image undermined like this is a serious matter; a strong self-image and the self-confidence that comes with it are the primary sources of the inner strength that is so essential for effective missionary service.

Crisis of Faith

Another dilemma many missionaries face is the crisis of faith some of their children go through during home leave or reentry. In the missionary world, you go abroad and come home not so much at the insistence of your employer but because the family has prayed about the matter and tried to discover God's will and plan. As your children struggle with reentry, in the ways discussed in chapter 4 and in the paragraphs below, they ask themselves—and you—how

God can be so unfeeling. In the private sector, the government, or the military, one can always blame the organization for moving people around, but how do you handle this query about God? What starts out as the child's crisis of faith can become yours as well, especially if your home leave or reentry, for some of the reasons already noted, isn't going smoothly either.

Longing for Home

One final issue you must confront is the inability of friends and loved ones to understand that you actually have a home overseas—and one, moreover, with which you probably identify more closely than the place you are visiting on home leave. As career missionaries, you normally put down deep roots in the foreign country, knowing that you and your children will be spending many years in this place. Your commitment to the host country and your involvement in all aspects of its life are much greater than that of the typical expatriate, even than that of foreign assistance volunteers (whose involvement may be deep but whose tour of duty is only two years). When you are on home leave, you miss your overseas home. Yet loved ones often cannot understand this grief and are not able to offer you any support or comfort. In the worst cases family and friends are threatened by your obvious longing for your overseas home and may criticize you for seeming to prefer the foreign country to your home. Surrounded by "loved ones," you may feel alienated, misunderstood, and alone.

Issues for Missionary Children

Third Culture Kids

Growing up in one or more foreign countries, the children of career missionaries belong to a unique population sometimes referred to as third culture kids (TCKs) or global nomads. Many of the children of diplomats, businesspeople, and military personnel also belong to this fraternity, which includes anyone who has grown up outside his or her passport country because of the career demands of one or both parents. As might be expected, these individuals are not altogether clear on where exactly home is. In some ways it is their passport country, the place where their parents were born and raised and where most of their relatives live, but in other ways home is that country or countries where these children spent their formative years—where they grew up, went to school, and made their best friends. Home is all of these places—and none of them. "Having spent a significant number of their developmental years in a culture other than their own," Pollock has written, "missionary kids have a sense of relationship to both host and home cultures. But they lack a sense of full membership in either" (1987a, 278).

In his book *Exile's Return*, Malcolm Cowley has described how people like this feel when they come "home."

> *If you came back, you wanted to leave again; if you went away, you longed to come back. Wherever you were, you could hear the call of the homeland, like the note of the herdsman's horn far away in the hills. You had one home out there and one over here, and yet you were an alien in both places. Your true abiding place was the vision of something very far off, and your soul was like the waves, always restless, forever in motion.* (117–18)

In the end, these individuals create their own home, that so-called third culture, which combines features of all of the cultures they have ever identified with. As Cowley suggests, it is not so much a location as a state of mind—a country of the heart—and in fact third culture children only feel truly at home not in any particular place but when they are in a gathering of other third-culture children. For those moments, at least, and among those people, they feel they belong.

The greatest difficulties for missionary children occur when it is time to return to their passport country to attend boarding school or university. While this return would be called reentry for most expatriates, for missionary children it is more of an entry, the first time they have come to live for an extended period in their nominal home culture. They are familiar with the culture, of course, having spent time there on one or more extended home leaves, but they have never really had to come to terms with it, knowing they would be going "home" at the end of the their parents' furlough. Now it is the parents who go home, leaving the child (usually a teenager) behind to make his or her way in an alien world.

Loss and Grief

Loneliness and homesickness are probably the most immediate problems the missionary child faces. "I found myself suddenly very homesick," one missionary teen remembers, "mostly for the people I know in my home country, and for that comfortable closeness I felt with those people. Here, upon reentry, I felt so completely alone." The loneliness of missionary children may be exacerbated because of the exceptional closeness of many missionary families. Unlike many of the other difficulties of reentry, this is one that friends and loved ones understand and can help the returnee work through.

Another related issue here is the dawning realization of loss, that the overseas home and people and one's entire way of life have disappeared, probably forever. With this loss comes grief, a grief which by and large the missionary child must endure alone. "[The] adjustment that caused me the most trouble and grief," one returnee observed, *was the great amount of loss and change I was forced to experience suddenly. The only thing that did not change in my life was a few pieces of clothing and a few articles I brought with me.... Everything else...was either altered or completely lost. Everything: people, relatives, friends, cars, climate, school, the dorm system, nature—Everything! It was almost as if I was (and I believe I was) dealing with thousands of deaths at once, including my own.*

A Question of Identity

Another issue teens and college-age missionary children confront is the need to suppress the most important part of their identity, that which is associated with their overseas experience. Other teens, their peers, cannot relate to the missionary's experiences, and it can be tedious to always have to explain oneself, filling people in on the context so they will understand the meaning of a story or a particular event. Moreover, many peers are either not interested in the missionary teen's experiences or are threatened by them and may become defensive or abusive. Beyond that the interests and values of the missionary child may be very different from those of peers, provoking the teenager to be cautious about revealing his or her feelings or opinions in conversation. Many missionary teens only reveal their true selves to other third culture children. As one teen noted,

People here just think so differently. I am always worrying about whether or not I am saying too much about my country. On the other hand, my peers all talk about their hometowns; yet, they all seem to understand each other. But they don't seem to be able to understand anything about where I come from, and the fact is they don't seem to even want to hear about it. So I feel I must be careful about what and how much I say.

The need to suppress whole parts of their identity only adds to the loneliness, alienation, and sense of loss many teens are already feeling. These teens know that they don't belong overseas anymore, and now they discover they don't really fit in at home either. "I feel as if my roots have been cut," one returning teen remembered, "and I don't know where I belong. I don't feel I belong in [my home country] right now. Yet in Malawi I don't have real roots [either]."

On Their Guard

The loneliness and isolation missionary teens feel is sometimes made worse by their own actions. Because they move so much—one observer estimates the typical missionary child lives in eight places in his or her first eighteen years—they learn to protect themselves from the pain of separation. After two or three wrenching relocations, most third culture children learn to be cautious about making emotional attachments that will only have to be broken a year or two down the road. They become self-sufficient, keep their distance in friendships, and are otherwise wary of personal commitments. While this makes separation easier, it does not make missionary children good candidates for friendship. When it comes time to go through reentry, when a friend could make all the difference and when separation is not in fact imminent, many third culture kids have lost the instinct for friendship. "Being a child," one third culture kid observed,

I had a child's ability to adjust. I learned to assume that things were only temporary, that upheavals were always around the corner. This enabled me to survive, of course, but in the process I learned not to trust in security, not to invest too much of myself in any one place for fear of losing it—in short, I learned to cultivate a sort of inner distance from the world around me. These are things I must unlearn today for they are handicaps to me as an adult trying to send down roots. But the habit and conviction of uninvolvement are very hard to break.

In their adult years, many third culture children lead restless lives, seemingly unable to put down roots or to trust fully in any roots they have put down. They move every few years almost out of habit, often with negative consequences for their careers. They expect periodic upheavals in their lives and usually manage to have them. In personal relationships, they are always preparing for the worst. "The loneliness some third culture kids experience," Pollock has observed,

is because they psychologically isolate themselves from other people and maintain the margin of safety in relationships, even in marriage. They think, "We can have a close relationship for the moment, but if you leave thirty seconds from now, I'll understand and I'll get on with my life." There is a distancing built into their lives and a preparation for letting go that is [not conducive to] building a long-term relationship. (1987b, 16)

What Missionaries and Their Children Can Do

Missionaries

In the end the accountability issue is as much a matter of educating the sponsoring public as it is making things happen overseas. This is not to say that you don't have to do any work if you are an articulate public speaker, but only that supporters often need help to understand and appreciate some of the less dramatic, long-term achievements that are the lot of many missionaries. Donors need to better understand the context in which you work, so that their expectations can be more realistic. In one setting building a church or making fifty converts might be a real possibility; in another just starting a youth group is probably overly ambitious. Supporters also need to learn how to appreciate results that cannot be counted or photographed, and you need to develop the knack of describing these results in ways that inspire the faithful.

For the spouse who is on the road there are no easy solutions. The usual suggestions here are for the traveling parent (1) to stay in close contact so that he or she is not forgotten and can still function as part of the family, (2) to return physically to the family as often as possible, and (3) for family members to go easy on each other when the absent parent returns. (The reader is referred to "Unaccompanied Tours," pages 164–67 for some relevant observations about family reunions.)

With regard to the problem of self-image, like all returnees, you should learn not to be so hard on yourself. A strong negative reaction to various aspects of life back in the home country is almost an inevitable consequence of any expatriate experience. Indeed, if you have adjusted at all to life overseas, then you are going to find home upsetting. And comparing your home culture unfavorably with that of your home abroad is, quite simply, human nature.

Finally, in the matter of people not understanding that you have a bona fide home overseas, one which you might miss very much during home leave, a useful response here is not to be surprised. Close friends and family members, however much they may try, will usually not be able to understand what it is like to live for many years abroad. They can be sympathetic and open-minded, but in the end it's not a question of sympathy or tolerance; it's a question of experience. Those who have not had this particular experience can never quite appreciate how you feel. The situation calls for patience and forgiveness.

Missionary Children

Most of the issues faced by missionary children lend themselves to solutions and interventions. Parents can do their children a great service during home leave by helping them establish ties with relatives and friends (including returned missionaries), which the children can then rely on when they come home for boarding school or university. Some churches have established a network of host homes throughout the country to provide support for teens, and others have established offices or stationed church representatives on select university campuses or in university towns—all for the purpose of alleviating the terrible loneliness many missionary teens feel.

For their part teens should seek out other missionary and third culture children like themselves, people in whose presence they can celebrate rather than suppress their cross-cultural identity. We have recommended this strategy for all returnees, but for missionary teens this is imperative, struggling as they are to somehow be themselves and yet still fit in to their home culture. "I very quickly found other MKs [missionary kids] on my campus," one teen noted. "They became my closest friends and support group, although we came from different countries.... If you are an MK, you are automatically accepted as a friend by other MKs, no questions asked." Another missionary teen observes that "only MKs can understand other MKs and fully comprehend their loss due to separation.... Parents try, but not even they can understand how deep our loss really is. New friends...can never replace MK friends who share common experiences and perceptions."

Missionary teens, like all returnees, must remember that feeling lonely and homesick, not fitting in—and not *wanting* to fit in—and not being understood are perfectly normal reactions to the experience of reentry. There is nothing wrong with them if they have these feelings; it's not that they are going about reentry all wrong or that they have made a terrible mistake. They have simply come home, which, it turns out, is not simple at all.

Epilogue

I went a little farther, he said. Then still a little farther—till
I had gone so far that I don't know how I'll ever get back.
—Joseph Conrad *Heart of Darkness*

We have stood so close to reentry for so many pages, poking into
every nook and cranny, that we might do well here in these closing moments to step back and place the whole experience once
again in perspective. While it can, indeed, be the trying, painful
transition chronicled herein, reentry also has its considerable plea-
sures and rewards, the majority of which have been left unexamined.

There was, of course, a certain method to our madness, a considered decision on our part to play down the positive side of
reentry—not because it is any less real or compelling than the
negative aspects, but only because most returnees correctly anticipate the nicer features of coming home and are not disappointed in this regard. It is the parts of reentry that you are not
expecting and are not ready for that prove to be troubling and
that you may need help with. And this is where we have chosen to
focus our attention.

But now it's time to be fair and restore some balance, to recall
that amidst the challenges, frustrations, and disappointments of

reentry there are interludes of great satisfaction and happiness—events and experiences that make you glad to be home, and moments when you wouldn't want to be anywhere else. They may be small moments—reunions with loved ones, visits to favorite places, returning to some pleasant old pastimes. Or they may be larger ones—when you tell a story that opens a friend's eyes in a way they've never been opened before; when you persuade a colleague, a boss, or perhaps an entire organization to change a practice or rethink a business strategy rule that is shortsighted or counterproductive; when someone is inspired by your example to go abroad and change his or her life forever.

There is also tremendous satisfaction and excitement in seeing one's own culture with new eyes, from the perspective of the foreign country. Whether you like or dislike what you see is not nearly as important as the gift of this new critical awareness, the ability to step outside your normal frame of reference and examine your behavior from a new vantage point. Many observers have noted that without such a vantage point, a place from which to observe, you can't really see your behavior—hence know yourself—at all.

As long as we're being fair about reentry, we might mention as well that there are many characteristics of life abroad that returnees do *not* miss, the blessed absence of which makes coming home all the more palatable. Many returnees gratefully dispense with being on display and under constant public scrutiny, having to struggle in a foreign language to make oneself understood or rely on interpreters, never quite trusting one's instincts, constantly entertaining, always being on the road (for the employee), the ever-present fear of offending others, having to put up with poor sanitation and unreliable communication and transportation systems, and doing without the many things you can't get and can't do in the host country. You will miss abroad acutely when you come home and may be overcome at times by a sense of longing, but in your lucid moments you will recall that even as you gazed wide-eyed and openmouthed at the majesty of the Himalayas or Victoria Falls, you felt yet another attack of diarrhea coming on.

The ultimate context for understanding and appreciating reentry has to be the overseas experience that precedes it, for this is what gives reentry its meaning. In this regard, we might remind ourselves that the word *reentry* comes to us from the space program, where, next to ignition or blastoff, the reentry phase is the most dangerous and difficult part of a space mission. In between, of course, comes the grand adventure of space exploration. So it is for the sojourner, whose reentry may also be dangerous and difficult but who needs only recall the wonder and richness of the overseas experience to put everything in perspective. Who can imagine astronauts, their space capsule rocking violently at the peak of reentry, wishing they'd never gone to the moon?

187

Useful Resources

American Field Service (AFS)
   198 Madison Avenue, 8th Floor
   New York, NY 10016 U.S.A.
   Phone: 212-299-9000
   www.afs.com
   high school exchange

Department of Defense Relocation Assistance Program
   Office of Educational Opportunities
   4015 Wilson Blvd. Suite 917
   Arlington, VA 22203 U.S.A.
   Phone: 703-696-5733
   military personnel and families

Foreign Service Youth Foundation
   PO Box 39185
   Washington, DC 20016 U.S.A.
   Phone: 301-404-6655
   teenagers, especially third culture kids

Global Nomad Resources
    1559 Scandia Circle, Suite 100
    Reston, VA 20190 U.S.A.
    Phone and Fax: 703-456-0566
    nmccaig@gmu.edu
    www.globalnomads.org
    teenagers, especially third culture kids and their families

Global Nomads, International
    2001 "O" Street, NW
    Washington, DC 20036 U.S.A.
    Phone: 202-466-2244
    info@gni.org
    www.globalnomadsassociation.com

    teenagers, especially third culture kids and their families

Interaction, Inc.
    PO Box 158
    Houghton, NY 14744-0158 U.S.A.
    Phone: 716-567-8774
    Fax: 716-567-4598
    75662,2070@compuserv.com ???
    www.tckinteract.net
    teenage and adult third culture kids, missionaries and families

"Letters"
    PO Box 90084
    Indianapolis, IN 46290-0084 U.S.A.
    Phone and Fax: 317-251-4933
    rdvanreken@aol.com
    http://members.aol.com/rdvanreken/
    missionaries and families

National Military Family Association
    6000 Stevenson Avenue, Suite 304
    Alexandria, VA 22304-3526 U.S.A.
    Phone: 703-823-6632
    www.nmfa.org
    military personnel and families

TCK World
    Phone: 915-672-8274
    sbritten@tckworld.com
    www.tckworld.com
    military and families, corporate and families, adult and teen-age third culture kids

Youth for Understanding
    3501 Newark Street NW
    Washington, DC 20016-3167 U.S.A.
    Phone: 202-966-6800
    e-mail@ncss.org
    high school exchange students

Bibliography

Adler, Nancy J. 1986. *International Dimensions of Organizational Behavior*. Belmont, CA: Wadsworth.

Austin, Clyde, ed. 1986. *Cross-Cultural Reentry: A Book of Readings*. Abilene, TX: Abilene Christian University.

Bachner, David. 1990. "Students of Four Decades: A Research Study of the Influences of an International Educational Exchange Experience on the Lives of German and U.S. High School Students." Washington, DC: Youth for Understanding.

Barich, Bill. 1984. *Traveling Light*. New York: Viking.

Becker, H., and A. L. Strauss. 1956. "Careers, Personality, and Adult Socialization." *American Journal of Sociology* 62, no. 3, November, 253–58.

Bennett, Janet. 1977. "Transition Shock: Putting Culture Shock in Perspective." *International and Intercultural Communication Annual IV*, December, 92–93.

Black, J. Stewart. 1991. "A Tale of Three Countries." Paper presented at the annual meeting of the Academy of Management, Miami.

Black, J. Stewart and Hal B. Gregersen. 1999. *So You're Going Home*. San Diego: Global Business Pubishers.

———. 1991. "When Yankee Comes Home: Factors Related to Expatriate and Spouse Repatriation Adjustment." *Journal of International Business Relations* 22, 4th Quarter, 671–93.

Black, J. Stewart, Hal B. Gregersen, and Mark E. Mendenhall. 1992. *Global Assignments: Successfully Expatriating and Repatriating International Managers*. San Francisco: Jossey-Bass.

Boley, Jean. 1986. "On the Art of Coming Home." In *Cross-Cultural Reentry: A Book of Readings*, edited by Clyde Austin. Abilene, TX: Abilene Christian University, 65–71.

Business Week. 1979. "How to Ease Reentry after Overseas Duty." 11 June, 82–83.

Cable, Mildred, and Francesca French. 1943. *The Gobi Desert*. London: Hodder and Stoughton.

Calvert, R. Jr. 1966. "The Returning Volunteer." *Annals of the American Academy of Political and Social Science,* no. 365, 105–18.

Clarke, K. 1978. "The Two-Way Street: A Survey of Volunteer Service Abroad." Wellington: New Zealand Council for Educational Research.

Council on Standards for International Educational Travel. 1994. Annual Report. Leesburg, VA.

Cowley, Malcolm. 1991. In *An Assessment of Reentry Issues of the Children of Missionaries,* by Doris L. Walters. New York: Vintage Press, 117–18.

Eakin, Kay Branaman. 1988. *The Foreign Service Teenager at Home in the United States*. Washington, DC: Foreign Service Institute/ Overseas Briefing Center.

English, Joseph T., and Joseph G. Colmen. 1963. "The United States Revisited: The Peace Corps Volunteer Returns." Washington, DC: Peace Corps.

Faulkner, Robert R., and Douglas B. McGaw. 1986. "Uneasy Homecoming: Stages in the Reentry Transition of Vietnam Veterans." In *Cross-Cultural Reentry: A Book of Readings*, edited by Clyde Austin. Abilene, TX: Abilene Christian University, 103–17.

Gellhorn, Martha. 1978. *Travels with Myself and Another*. London: Allen Lane.

"Global Relocation Trends 1999 Survey Report." 1999. New York: Windham International.

Grove, Cornelius. 1989. *Orientation Handbook for Youth Exchange Programs*. Yarmouth, ME: Intercultural Press.

Harris, Louis, and Associates. 1969. "A Survey of Returned Peace Corps Volunteers." New York: Louis Harris et al.

Hunter, Victor. 1986. "Closure and Commencement: The Stress of Finding Home." In *Cross-Cultural Reentry: A Book of Readings*, edited by Clyde Austin. Abilene, TX: Abilene Christian University, 179–89.

Kendall, Daniel W. 1981. "Repatriation: An Ending and a Beginning." *Business Horizons* 24, 21–25.

Killen, Mary. 1997. "Your Problems Solved." *The Spectator*, 29 March, 63.

Koehler, Nancy. 1986. "Reentry Shock." In *Cross-Cultural Reentry: A Book of Readings*, edited by Clyde Austin. Abilene, TX: Abilene Christian University, 89–94.

La Brack, Bruce. 1993. "Re-entry in a Business Context." *Nipporica Notes* 2, no. 3, October, 1–2.

Lewis, C. S. 1965. *Out of the Silent Planet*. New York: Macmillan.

Longworth, Sam. 1986. "The Returned Volunteer: A Perspective." In *Cross-Cultural Reentry: A Book of Readings*, edited by Clyde Austin. Abilene, TX: Abilene Christian University, 85.

Marquardt, Michael J., and Dean W. Engel. 1993. *Global Human Resource Development*. Englewood Cliffs, NJ: Prentice Hall.

Martin, Judith N. 1986. "Communication in the Intercultural Reentry: Student Sojourners' Perceptions of Change in Reentry Relationship." *International Journal of Intercultural Relations* 9, no. 1, 14.

———. 1984. "The Intercultural Reentry: Conceptualization and Directions for Future Research." *International Journal of Intercultural Relations* 8, no. 2, 115–33.

McClure, Karen. 1988. "Children and the Expatriate Lifestyle." *Expatriate Observer* 11, no. 4, October, 1–5.

McCluskey, Karen Curnow, ed. 1994. *Notes from a Traveling Childhood*. Washington, DC: Foreign Service Youth Foundation.

Miller, Marcia. 1988. "Reflections on Reentry after Teaching in China." *Occasional Papers in Intercultural Learning* 14, December. New York: AFS Center for the Study of Intercultural Learning.

Moran, Stahl and Boyer. 1989. "Repatriation Practices of American Multinational Corporations." Paper presented at the annual conference of the Society for International Education, Training and Research, May.

Naipaul, V. S. 1987. *An Area of Darkness*. New York: Penguin.

New York Times. 1985. 14 October.

Olsen, Gaila Hagg. 1985. "Returned Peace Corps Volunteers: Can They Go Home Again?" Unpublished research paper.

Osland, Joyce Sautters. 1995. *The Adventure of Working Abroad: Hero Tales from the Global Frontier*. San Francisco: Jossey-Bass.

Oster, Patrick. 1993. "The Fast Track Leads Overseas." *Business Week*, 1 November, 64–68.

Pascoe, Robin. 2000. *Homeward Bound: A Spouse's Guide to Repatriation*. Vancouver: Expatriate Press.

———. 1992. *The Wife's Guide to Successful Living Abroad*. Singapore: Times Books International.

Pollock, David. 1987a. "Welcome Home! Easing the Pain of MK Reentry." *Evangelical Missions Quarterly* 23, 278–83.

———. 1987b. "Reaching Out to Third Culture Kids." *Trans World Radio* 8, no. 5, November/December, 15–19.

Pusch, Margaret. 1988. "Reentry Is Going Home." Washington, DC: National Association for Foreign Student Affairs.

Rohrlich, Beulah F., and Judith N. Martin. 1991. "Host Country and Reentry Adjustment of Student Sojourners." *International Journal of Intercultural Relations* 15, no. 2, 163–82.

Rosenblum, Mort. 1989. "Back Home." *American Way*, 15 December, 74–80.

Schuetz, Alfred. 1945. "The Homecomer." *American Journal of Sociology* 50, 369–76.

Shepard, Steven. 1998. *Managing Cross-Cultural Transition*. Bayside, NY: Alethia Publications.

Siebenaler, Rita. 1988. "Re-entry: A Family Crisis." *Foreign Service Journal*, June, 52–53.

Smith, Lee. 1975. "The Hazards of Coming Home." *Dun's Review*, October, 71–73.

Society for Human Resource Management. 1992. "1992 SHRM/Commerce Clearing House Survey." Chicago: Commerce Clearing House Inc.

Sobie, Jane Hipkins. 1986. "The Culture Shock of Coming Home Again." In *Cross-Cultural Reentry: A Book of Readings*, edited by Clyde Austin. Abilene TX: Abilene Christian University, 95–101.

Spurling, Hilary. 1990. *Paul Scott: A Life*. London: Hutchinson.

Sussman, Nan M. 1986. "Reentry Research and Training: Methods and Implications." *International Journal of Intercultural Relations* 10, no. 2, 235–54.

Theant, Roger, Daniel Kealey, and Francis Hawes. 1979. "Reentry: A Guide for Returning Home." Québec: Canadian International Development Agency.

Tung, Rosalie. 1988. *The New Expatriates*. Cambridge, MA: Ballinger.

United States Department of Defense. 1994. "Worldwide Manpower Distribution by Geographical Area." Washington, DC: Washington Headquarters Services, Directorate for Information Operations and Reports, 30 September.

United States Department of Defense. 1994. *Defense 94*. Alexandria, VA: American Forces Information Service.

USA Today. 1995. 8 November, front page.

Wallach, Joel, and Gail Metcalf. (No date available.) "Ten Minutes Out—For Those about to Return Home." American Association of Malaysia.

Walters, Doris L. 1991. *An Assessment of Reentry Issues of the Children of Missionaries*. New York: Vintage Press.

Weaver, Gary. 1987. "The Process of Reentry." *Advising Quarterly* 2, Fall, 1–9.

Werkman, Sidney. 1986. "Coming Home: Adjustment of Americans to the United States after Living Abroad." In *Cross-Cultural Re-*

entry: A Book of Readings, edited by Clyde Austin. Abilene TX: Abilene Christian University, 5–17.

———. 1979. "Coming Home: Adjustment Problems of Adolescents Who Have Lived Overseas." *Adolescent Psychiatry* 8, 178–89.

———. 1975. "Over Here and Back There: American Adolescents Overseas." *Foreign Service Journal* 52, March, 13–15, 30.

White, Merry. 1988. *The Japanese Overseas: Can They Go Home Again?* New York: Free Press.

Williams, Lorna V. 1986. "When Overseas Managers Return." *American Way*, 1 November, 32–36.

Wilson, Angene H. 1993. "A Cross-National Perspective on Reentry of High School Exchange Students." *International Journal of Intercultural Relations* 17, no. 4, 465–92.

Winslow, E. A. 1977. "A Survey of Returned Peace Corps Volunteers." Washington, DC: Peace Corps.

Youth for Understanding. 1987. "Going Home Again: The Reentry Process." *Horizons*. Washington, DC.

Index

Other Craig Storti titles published by
Intercultural Press and Nicholas Brealey Publishing

The Art of Crossing Cultures

Cross-Cultural Dialogues: 74 Brief Encounters with Cultural Difference

Figuring Foreigners Out: A Practical Guide

and,

Old World/New World: Bridging Cultural Differences: Britain, France, Germany, and the U.S.